The United Nations
and Rhodesia

Ralph Zacklin

The Praeger Special Studies program—utilizing the most modern and efficient book production techniques and a selective worldwide distribution network—makes available to the academic, government, and business communities significant, timely research in U.S. and international economic, social, and political development.

The United Nations and Rhodesia
A Study in International Law

PRAEGER SPECIAL STUDIES IN INTERNATIONAL POLITICS AND GOVERNMENT

Praeger Publishers   New York   Washington   London

Library of Congress Cataloging in Publication Data

Zacklin, Ralph.
　　The United Nations and Rhodesia.

　　(Praeger special studies in international politics
and government)
　　　1.　United Nations—Rhodesia, Southern.
2.　Sanctions (International law)　I.　Title.
JX1977.2.R5Z33　　　　341.23'689'1　　　　74-1751
ISBN 0-275-09260-7

PRAEGER PUBLISHERS
111 Fourth Avenue, New York, N.Y. 10003, U.S.A.
5, Cromwell Place, London SW7 2JL, England

Published in the United States of America in 1974
by Praeger Publishers, Inc.

To Lyda, Joseph, and Elias

ACKNOWLEDGMENTS

In the preparation of this study, I was fortunate to have had at my disposal the research and library facilities of the Carnegie Endowment and the United Nations in New York. For reasons beyond my control, the research and writing of this study were compressed into the relatively short period between March and August 1973. Without the dedicated support and collaboration of some of my colleagues, this study might never have been completed. I particularly wish to acknowledge the assistance of Mrs. Vivian Hewitt and Mrs. Jane Lowenthal of the Carnegie Endowment library for the admirable way in which they assembled the primary and secondary sources upon which this study is based.

Special thanks must go to Miss Jane Flood for the competent manner in which she assumed the administrative and secretarial burdens associated with the study and for the valuable research functions which she performed, and to Mrs. Catherine Kubiak who volunteered her assistance when it was most needed.

R. Z.

Crises are both a challenge and an opportunity for international institutions. Indeed, it may be argued that much of the constitutional development of the United Nations since 1945 has been generated by events of the most critical nature such as Kashmir, Korea, Suez, the Congo, and Rhodesia.

Viewed from the perspective of its impact on international law and international institutions and the interaction between international and national jurisdictions, the Rhodesian crisis offers an extraordinarily varied foundation for the examination of the past and present performance and future prospects of the international legal order.

The special significance of the Rhodesian crisis stems from its dual characteristics as both an international problem of concern to the society of nations and a domestic problem of primary concern to the metropolitan power. The Charter of the United Nations establishes a basic distinction in Article 2, paragraph 7, between "matters which are essentially within the domestic jurisdiction of any state" and those which are not—a distinction which it might be thought is unexceptionable in an organization based on the principle of the sovereign equality of all its members but which, as history and the practice of the organization have revealed, is increasingly difficult to maintain. When the internal, domestic system of law and government in a state or territory is overturned, when its executive, legislative, and judicial organs are imperiled or overthrown, when respect for the most elementary human rights is abandoned, the repercussions within an increasingly interdependent international community are not easily contained. Moreover, the breakdown of domestic constitutional law creates a vacuum which, in a particular context, international law and international institutions alone may fill. Rhodesia is, in this respect, a paradigm case.

At the basis of the international community's encroachment upon matters of "domestic" concern is the realization and the conviction that the denial of fundamental human rights, wherever it occurs, is ultimately a threat to international peace and security. It is an indication of the evolution of international law and international institutions that the once rigid distinction between matters of domestic and international concern is gradually being eroded, particularly with respect to gross violations of human rights and racial discrimination.

The unilateral declaration of independence (UDI) by a white, racialist minority for the purpose of perpetuating minority rule over a disenfranchised but predominantly African population is not only a clear breach of domestic constitutional law (that is, of the British Crown) but also a violation of and a challenge to established principles of international public policy underwritten by international law in general and enacted in the Charter of the United Nations in particular.*

The present study seeks to explore the Rhodesian crisis from the perspective of its impact on international law and international institutions and the interaction between international and national jurisdictions.

Part I of the study places Rhodesia in its historical context, in relationship to British colonial policy in both the nineteenth and twentieth centuries and to the evolution of international law and institutions throughout this same period.

Part II examines the formulation of the policy of international sanctions and the principal political, legal, and institutional issues involved. Part III is devoted to an examination of the continuing enforcement of sanctions—through the actions of the executive, legislative, and judicial branches of states and through the creation of international machinery.

In undertaking a study of this kind, it is impossible not to remain conscious that the drama is still unfolding. However, an attempt has been made to view events with detachment and to place them in the larger canvas which we have established. In so doing, it is hoped that the study will contribute to a deeper understanding of the Rhodesian problem and the relevance of international law and international institutions to a solution of that problem.

---

*The most frequently cited examples of principles of a public policy character include the prohibition on the threat or use of force, the prohibition of genocide, the prohibition of racial discrimination, and the principles contained in Articles 1 and 2 of the Charter of the United Nations. For an examination of the international public policy connotations implicit in the Rhodesian case, see Ralph Zacklin, "Challenge of Rhodesia," International Conciliation No. 575, November 1969.

CONTENTS

The extraordinary domestic and international juridical-political imbroglio created by the Rhodesian unilateral declaration of independence (UDI) of November 11, 1965 is, on the one hand, a product of history and British colonial policy and, on the other hand, a reflection of the limitations of the contemporary international legal order and the United Nations organization. Until the final hour, Britain maintained that the question of Southern Rhodesia was a "domestic" matter; in so doing, she was internally consistent in her interpretation of Article 2, paragraph 7, of the Charter and in this respect did not differ from any other colonial power in the United Nations.[1] The United Nations, when finally seized of the problem, not unexpectedly, was unable to reconcile rhetoric and reality.

Geopolitical factors have played an important role in the historical and constitutional evolution of Rhodesia, and in the years since UDI have unquestionably determined the continued existence of the Smith regime. Rhodesia (Southern Rhodesia) is situated between Zambia (formerly Northern Rhodesia) in the north and the Transvaal (South Africa) in the south; it has a common frontier with Botswana (the former British protectorate of Bechuanaland) in the west and Mozambique, a Portuguese-held colonial territory, in the east. The tacit support of the regimes, which control the territories to the south and east of Rhodesia, is, as we shall see below, of crucial importance both with regard to Rhodesia's ability to withstand economic sanctions and in analyzing the strategy of sanctions as formulated by the Security Council. Rhodesia, 150,820 square miles in area, has a population of 5,590,000, of whom 5,335,000 are Africans and 255,000 (4.56 percent of the total population) Europeans.[2]

In viewing the Rhodesian crisis in historical perspective, it is important to bear in mind what may be termed temporal values. The prevailing values of the late nineteenth century or early twentieth

3

century in world affairs were, of course, quite different from what they are today or what they were even a quarter of a century ago in such matters as acquisition of territory, sovereign equality, and self-determination. The Victorian community of nations differed both quantitatively and qualitatively from contemporary society. International law reflected both in form and substance the narrower and more parochial conception of so-called civilized, mainly European, nations and, apart from the creation of some minor administrative unions in the field of communications, the world was still in the Stone Age so far as general, political international organizations were concerned.

The British penetration and ultimate colonization of Rhodesia may be traced to the year 1888 and the vision and ambition of Cecil John Rhodes. In the late nineteenth century, British rule in southern Africa was centered upon the Cape Colony. Rhodes, an immigrant to the Cape in 1870, had amassed a considerable fortune from diamond mining in Kimberley and by the late 1880s was eager to devote his attention to what had become a consuming passion—the extension of the British Empire and its "civilizing influence" to as large a portion of the globe as possible. British imperialism during this era was, in George Orwell's view, "sentimental, ignorant, and dangerous," but it was, he added, still possible to be an imperialist and a gentle-man.[3] The collected papers of George Orwell do not reveal whether it was his view that all imperialists could be gentlemen or whether this was distinctly a British trait.

Rhodes, there can be no doubt, was an imperialist, a man of forceful personality and great ability in the execution of his visionary schemes. His most grandiose scheme was the establishment of a domain under British rule stretching from the Cape to Cairo. To Rhodes it seemed logical to extend British influence north from the Cape Colony to the "unclaimed" territories of central Africa.

The chief obstacles to such a scheme were twofold. First, a growing rivalry was developing among the European powers in Africa and an unseemly, indeed ungentlemanly, scramble for "unclaimed" territory was taking place. The territorial object of this rivalry among the powers consisted largely of lands in central Africa which, until the 1880s, had remained virtually unexplored. The territorial pretentions of France, Portugal, and Germany and the machinations of King Leopold II of Belgium must have appeared more than a little alarming to Rhodes. Against this background Bismarck convoked the Berlin Conference of 1884-85. Officially, the 14-power discussions were devoted to free trade and free navigation in the Congo and the Niger, the formalities to be observed in the annexation of African territory, the protection of the native peoples, and suppression of the slave trade.[4] Although it had no mandate to deal with territorial

4

questions as such, in fact this was the principal albeit unpublicized business of the Conference: "It was an unquestioned assumption at Berlin that the European Powers had the right to annex African territory for their own advantage, so long as the nominal consent of a certain number of African chiefs had been obtained."[5]

It is interesting to observe the extent to which the European powers sought to preserve the appearance, if not the substance, of the international legality of their acts. A great deal of emphasis was placed on obtaining the formal consent of African chiefs (pacta sunt servanda), although whether and to what extent these chiefs actually understood the treaties to which they subscribed, and the nature of the "substantial considerations" by which such consent was obtained, hardly bears close examination. Similarly, in the writings of the time, there are repeated references to the capacity of the African chiefs to enter into agreements with the European powers. Particularly illuminating in this context is Stanley's description of the African chiefs, some 450 of whom had entered into treaties with King Leopold's Association Internationale du Congo (AIC),[6] and

> whose rights would be conceded by all to have been indisputable, since they held their lands by undisturbed occupation, by long ages of succession, by real divine right. Of their own free will, without coercion, but for substantial considerations . . . they had transferred their rights of sovereignty and of ownership to the Association.[7]

Stanley's concern for the legal proprieties of undisturbed occupation, long ages of succession, and divine right is very appealing. The Berlin Conference was noticeably cooler, however, to the British suggestion that norms should be established for the annexation of territory. As C. H. Alexandrowicz has pointed out, the General Act of Berlin which issued from the Conference "confined the application of its two most important principles, i.e., the principle of notification and the principle of effective occupation, to the coasts of the African Continent."[8]

A British proposal that these rules be extended from coastal areas to the whole of Africa was rejected on the disingenuous ground that too little was known about the interior of Africa.

The second obstacle to Rhodes' scheme was, if anything, even more tangible than the first. Although the European powers referred a great deal to "unclaimed" territories, what they really meant was African territory that had not been claimed by European powers. Alexandrowicz has concluded on the basis of his exhaustive historical research that in the nineteenth century the African Continent could not have under any circumstances been considered territorium nullius. It has since millenia been covered by a network of State organizations and Empires of a great diversity which revealed at the same time some similarities and even traces of unity.[9]

Directly in the path of Rhodes' planned expansion lay the lands of the Amandebele tribe ruled by Chief Lo Bengula. In January 1888, Rhodes learned that the Chief had signed a "treaty" with the Transvaal Boers to the south. John Moffat, an agent of the British High Commissioner in South Africa, prevailed upon the Chief to rescind this "treaty" in favor of an agreement wherein Lo Bengula consented not to make any agreements with foreign states or cede any land "without the previous knowledge and sanction of Her Majesty's High Commissioner for South Africa."[10] Having thus obtained a right of first refusal, so to speak, the next step was to extract from Lo Bengula specific property rights. In October Lo Bengula conceded, by the so-called Rudd Concession, exclusive mining rights in his domains to Rhodes. In consideration for these rights, the Chief, his successors, and heirs were to receive 100 pounds per month in perpetuity, 1,000 rifles, ammunition, and, as the pièce de résistance, an armed steamboat on the Zambezi River. The concession and the nature of the consideration involved were probably fairly typical of the time and could not be considered in any way repugnant to international law. Indeed, as may be observed, the forms of international treaty making were scrupulously observed, and however unequal the agreement may seem to the contemporary observer, nineteenth-century international law undoubtedly sanctioned the arrangement. The concession was formulated, however, in such a manner as to amount to a virtual surrender of sovereignty. Realizing his error, Lo Bengula attempted to cancel the concession, but it was too late.[11]

Armed with the Rudd Concession, Rhodes sought permission to form a company under Royal Charter for the purpose of developing the resources of the territory. The chartered company was an extremely useful and economical device much favored by nineteenth-century British governments since it permitted the government to expand its territorial competence without necessarily exposing itself to either political opprobium, financial risk, or the military implications. After some intensive lobbying by Rhodes in London, a Royal Charter of incorporation was granted to the British South Africa Company on October 29, 1889. The Charter authorized the Company "to acquire by any concession, agreement, grant, or treaty, all or any rights, interests, authorities, jurisdictions, and powers of any kind or nature whatever, including powers necessary for the purposes of government, and the preservation of public order."[12] The sweeping, quasi-governmental powers granted to the Company left no doubt as to the intentions of the British government or the ultimate fate of the local ruler.

A treaty of June 11, 1891 between Great Britain and Portugal delimited the eastern frontier of the territories under the Company's administration and in the same year an Order in Council conferred upon the High Commissioner for South Africa the power to exercise jurisdiction over the territory in the name of Queen Victoria.[13] The last remaining vestiges of Lo Bengula's authority were soon eliminated. After a brief struggle with European settlers in 1893-94, Lo Bengula died. We can but agree with Alexandrowicz when he states:

> While the leading African Rulers must have welcomed the chance of entry of their countries into the wider (universal) Family of Nations and the prospect of benefits to be derived from industrial progress, and while a temporary control of their external sovereignty was possibly instrumental in effecting such entry, the excessive interference of European Powers with their internal sovereignty and their legal customs and traditions was not a constructive factor.[14]

Indeed, it is probably an understatement.

The fact that international law was one of the instruments by which indigenous African authority was subverted might, at first sight, appear incongruous, but this is to fail to understand the nature and function of international law. International law has always been a system of norms, more or less well-defined governing relations between states or entities possessing some degree of international personality. On one level, the system operates as an international law of cooperation,[15] but at a different level, it operates as a mechanism for coexistence or reconciliation of opposing ideologies or civilizations. Historically this may be observed in the struggle between Christianity and Islam many centuries ago or in the contemporary East-West ideological conflict. The role of international law in the establishment of relations between European powers and African rulers in the nineteenth century must be seen then as an example of the international law of coexistence despite the inherent disparities in the relationship. This relationship, projected forward some 80 years, has today given rise to one of the major influences on the renovation of international law. The qualitative impact of the newly independent states on the entire fabric of international law is, unquestionably, imminent in a number of important substantive areas such as the law of the sea and the law of international trade and investment.

But there is another aspect of this incongruity that requires explanation. Since the relationship between the European powers and Africa in the nineteenth century was so obviously unequal and since the designs of the European powers were so openly annexationist, whether by guile or by force, was this not contrary to some of the fundamental principles of international law? The answer, of course, lies in a temporal view of international law. Nineteenth-century international law did not prohibit the use of force, nor did it prescribe the territorial integrity or political independence of any state. These fundamental principles developed much later, and even today the existence of international rules of jus cogens gives rise to considerable debate.16 The fact is that international law condoned and provided the formal framework for the dissolution of the various colonial regimes.

Lo Bengula's death removed from the scene the chief link in the relations established between the Amandebele Tribe and Rhodes. Shortly thereafter, an Order in Council of 1898 extended the area under Company rule and established a governmental regime for the territory known as Rhodesia.17 The first legislature consisted of four elected members and five nominees of the Company. Native (African) affairs were reserved to the imperial government in London, but with respect to other matters the European inhabitants of Rhodesia, unlike many other colonies, enjoyed a substantial measure of inde-pendence from British control—a characteristic which would be accentuated and would have considerable significance in the ensuing years.

NOTES

1. On the concept of domestic jurisdiction in United Nations practice, see Rosalyn Higgins, The Development of International Law through the Political Organs of the United Nations, Oxford University Press, London, 1963. See, in particular, Part II, pp. 58-130.

2. 1973 World Almanac and Book of Facts. The population figures are a 1971 government estimate and therefore open to some doubt. While the Rhodesian government wishes to maintain the image of a stable European population in proportion to the total population of the country, an examination of the available statistics indicates a relative decrease in the size of the European population since UDI.

3. The Collected Essays, Journalism and Letters of George Orwell, Secker and Warburg, London, 1961, Vol. I, p. 160.

4. See Ruth Slade, King Leopold's Congo, Oxford University Press, London, 1962.

5. Ibid., p. 41.

6. This Association must rank as one of the great political public relations exercises of all time. Leopold II foresaw the great commercial benefits to be derived from colonization of the Congo, and profiting from British disinterest, he formed the AIC. By brilliant use of what would today be called public relations, he managed to persuade Europe that the AIC was a small, philanthropic, altruistic, and essentially humanitarian organization aimed at suppressing the slave trade and introducing legitimate commerce into the Congo Basin—all of which was true. It was also true that in July 1885, Leopold II was proclaimed Sovereign of the Congo Independent State acting in a purely personal capacity. Leopold was, therefore, absolute sovereign over a land he had never seen and would never visit. The only limitations on his authority were those of international public opinion and the vague prescriptions of the Berlin Act. See Slade, op. cit., pp. 42-43.

7. H. M. Stanley, The Congo and the Founding of Its Free State, Sampson Low, London, 1885, Vol. II, pp. 379-380.

8. C. H. Alexandrowicz, The European African Confrontation: A Study in Treaty Making, A. W. Sijthoff, Leiden, 1973.

9. Ibid.

10. British and Foreign State Papers, Vol. 79, pp. 868-869.

11. "Did you ever see a chameleon catch a fly?" Lo Bengula asked the missionary Helm. "The chameleon gets behind the fly and remains motionless for some time, then he advances very slowly and gently, first putting forward one leg and then another. At last, when well within reach, he darts his tongue and the fly disappears. England is the chameleon and I am that fly." Reported by Sir Sydney Shippard to Sir Hercules Robinson, as cited in P. Mason, The Birth of a Dilemma, Oxford University Press, London, 1958, p. 105.

12. Paragraph 3. For the full text of the Royal Charter, see Edward Hertslet, The Map of Africa by Treaty, 3rd ed., Cass, London, 1967, Vol. I, pp. 271-277.

13. "British and Foreign State Papers," Vol. 83, p. 27, and Hertslet's Treaties, Vol. 19, p. 30.

14. Alexandrowicz, op. cit.

15. See Wolfgang Friedmann, The Changing Structure of International Law, Stevens, London, 1964, pp. 60-67.

16. For a survey of international legal doctrine with respect to jus cogens, see the excellent working paper prepared by Erik Suy for the conference organized by the Carnegie Endowment at Lagonissi in 1966 in "Papers and Proceedings of the Lagonissi Conference," Vol. II, pp. 17-77.

17. See Hertslet's Treaties, op. cit., p. 268.

2

THE SACRED TRUST
OF CIVILIZATION

The carnage of World War I gave way to the false dawn of a new world order incorporated in a series of international agreements and consecrated in the creation of the League of Nations. The most important of the international agreements relating to Africa which had been concluded prior to 1914—including the Convention on the Revision of the General Act of Berlin, 1885 and the General Act and Declaration of Brussels, 1890—were revised and incorporated in the instruments signed at St. Germain-en-Laye in 1919. In so doing, the European powers endorsed the principles which, in the course of the late nineteenth and early twentieth centuries, had gradually evolved in relation to dependent areas. H. Duncan Hall, in his book Mandates, Dependencies and Trusteeship, identified these principles as follows:

1. the maintenance of peace through a concert of the powers;
2. recognition of the dual mandate principle—that is, trusteeship for dependent peoples involved duties toward the peoples under trust and obligations toward the family of nations which had a collective responsibility in the matter;
3. recognition that duties to backward peoples (sic) form a suitable subject matter for international law;
4. acknowledgment of the necessity of establishing common international rules and standards;
5. the desirability of permanent machinery for coordination and supervision of such rules and standards.1

It is clear then that, with the exception of the establishment of international machinery, the main elements of the mandate system that emerged from the Paris Peace Conference formed part of customary or conventional international law prior to the Covenant of the League of Nations and possibly as early as 1885. In the light of the arguments advanced more than 70 years later by those opposed to self-determination or those for whom such questions were matters of domestic jurisdiction, it is not without interest that such principles as collective responsibility and the recognition that duties toward dependent peoples constituted a proper subject matter of international law formed part of the international legal order at the turn of the century.

Article 22 of the Covenant of the League of Nations provided for a three-tier system of mandates for territories detached from Turkey and Germany at the conclusion of World War I. According to the stage of development of the territory concerned, it was classified as either an A, B, or C mandate. The Covenant of the League of Nations envisaged an early existence as an independent nation for A mandates. The main differences between B and C mandates were that C mandates could be administered by the mandatory as an integral part of its metropolitan territory, and the open-door provisions of the B mandates were omitted from C mandates.[2] The system was based upon the principle that "the well-being and development of such peoples form a sacred trust of civilization." A Permanent Mandates Commission was established to receive and examine annual reports of the mandatory powers, and the right of the inhabitants of mandated territories to petition the League was recognized.[3] Although history's judgment of the mandate system is, on the whole, positive, the philosophy and underlying ambivalence of the system aroused considerable hostility in some quarters where it was viewed as an example of European neocolonialism and a thinly veiled annexation. The distinguished British historian H. A. L. Fisher commented that "the crudity of conquest was draped in the veil of morality."[4] Historians more generally, however, regard the mandate system as a Wilsonian triumph and one of the most successful achievements of the League.[5]

Inasmuch as the mandate system constituted an overt internationalization of the principles of dependent rule with regard to former German and Turkish colonies, it was reasonable to suppose that the same principles applied mutatis mutandis to nonmandated territories. What was the relationship between mandated and nonmandated treatment? Were the same criteria and standards to be applied? How, if at all, did the international obligations of the mandatory states differ with respect to territories under mandate and other dependencies? The implications of the mandate system for the British and French colonial systems were quite clear. In particular, if the mandated territories were considered by the international community as subjects of international concern, it was very difficult to argue that nonmandated territories should be of any less international concern. Faced with this dilemma, Britain and France, under pressure from the United States, agreed to the insertion in the Covenant of Article 23 (b), according to which the members of the League were to "undertake to secure just treatment of the native inhabitants of

11

territories under their control." Article 23 (b), however, remained a dead letter.6

Constitutional and related developments in Rhodesia in the 1920s and 1930s were in sharp contrast to the rhetoric of the Covenant and the principles embodied in the mandate system. Indeed, these principles were observed more in their breach than in their observance as the position of the European minority was systematically consolidated.

In 1922 a referendum was organized by the British government in Rhodesia to determine whether the Europeans there wished to become a part of South Africa or to remain separate. There were 34,000 Europeans in Rhodesia at the time, and they voted 8,774 to 5,989 to remain separate. Rhodesia was formally annexed to the British Crown on September 12, 1923 and, under Letters Patent of October 1, 1923, achieved self-government.

The 1923 Constitution reserved certain powers to the British government. The laudable intent of the reserve powers—the protection of African interests—was, however, implemented in strange ways. The 1930 Land Apportionment Act, for example, which became the legal basis for Rhodesia's social and racial structure, was enacted without interference from London notwithstanding its flagrant discrimination against Africans. Under the rule of the British South Africa Company, special reserves had been established exclusively for Africans, but until 1930 it had been possible for anyone, including Africans, to purchase land outside the reserves. There was, of course, an enormous disproportion in land ownership by Europeans and Africans. By 1925 some 31 million acres of land had been purchased by Europeans and a mere 45,000 acres by Africans. But the purchase of land by Africans anywhere in the country was considered to be a source of possible friction between the African and European communities, and the Rhodesian Chief Native Commissioner Herbert J. Taylor recommended that special areas be set aside near the reserves for land purchases by Africans only. The British Colonial Secretary (who at that time was Winston Churchill) refused to take action immediately, preferring to act on the recommendations of a so-called impartial commission of inquiry. In 1925 the Morris Carter Commission was asked to study the practicability of limiting the acquisition of land according to race. Its conclusions followed closely the earlier recommendations of the Native Commissioner, and the language of the Commission's report scarcely attempted to conceal its outright racial discrimination (Carter Commissioner Report, Salisbury, 1926).

The ensuing Land Apportionment Act of 1930 divided the country into native areas, European areas, and unallocated lands. The Africans were allocated about 33 percent of the land and the Europeans 50 percent including the urban areas. As a result of the Act, Africans were restricted to rural areas and could not own property or even occupy

12

premises in the towns. The severity of the racial segregation created by the Act may be judged by the fact that some 30 years later, a special amendment to the law was required to enable African students to live on the site of the University College in Salisbury. In theory, the purpose of the Land Apportionment Act was to prevent the wholesale alienation of land to Europeans, but the method chosen for achieving this goal, by segregation of Africans and Europeans, killed any hope of achieving a multiracial and egalitarian society. The Act rapidly came to be regarded by Europeans as a guarantee of their privileged position and by the Africans as the basis of racial segregation and discrimination.

The franchise under the 1923 Constitution did not, theoretically, discriminate against Africans, but in practice, the property and educational qualifications were such that the overwhelming majority of Africans were unable to qualify for the franchise within the foreseeable future. In 1953 when the Federation of Rhodesia and Nyasaland was formed, there were still fewer than 450 Africans on the electoral roll. (At the time of the creation of the Federation, the Rhodesian electoral roll contained 47,533 Europeans, 535 Asians, 535 colored people, and 429 Africans. No African had ever been elected to the legislature.)

NOTES

1. H. Duncan Hall, Mandates, Dependencies and Trusteeship, Stevens, London, 1948; Kraus Reprint Co., New York, 1972, p. 105.

2. See further H. Duncan Hall, op. cit., pp. 149 ff.

3. Ibid., pp. 197-210.

4. H. A. L. Fisher, A History of Europe, Houghton-Mifflin, Co., Boston, 1936, Vol. III, p. 1207.

5. H. Duncan Hall, op. cit., p. 115.

6. Ibid., p. 224.

3

THE EMERGENCE
OF THE THIRD WORLD

When the Charter of the United Nations was drafted in San Francisco, Article 23 (b) of the Covenant was transformed into Chapter XI of the Charter: the Declaration Regarding Nonselfgoverning Territories. It was described by the late Ralph Bunche as an international charter of colonial administration.[1] Chapter XI differs fundamentally from Chapters XII and XIII (which deal with trusteeship) in that it establishes the principle of international accountability without, however, providing for machinery of supervision. The specific obligations incumbent upon member states under Article 73 of the Charter include

1. the obligation to ensure the "political, economic, social, and educational advancement" of the inhabitants;

2. the obligation "to develop self-government, to take due account of the political aspirations of the peoples, and to assist them in the progressive development of their free political institutions"; and

3. the obligation to transmit to the Secretary-General for information purposes information of a technical nature relating to economic, social, and educational conditions in the territories.

The first session of the United Nations General Assembly faced the problem of defining nonselfgoverning territories—a highly ambiguous concept even by Charter standards. This was, of course, only another installment in the lengthy United Nations saga of drawing the line between international and domestic jurisdiction. The provisions of Article 73 were considered applicable, from the time the Charter entered into force, to all territories that had been administered under League mandates or for which at some future time trusteeship agreements might be negotiated. The real problem, however, concerned territories such as Rhodesia, which had been "self-governing" according to domestic constitutional law since 1923 but which for the vast majority of its peoples continued to manifest all the characteristics of a nonselfgoverning territory.

The General Assembly debate revealed, not unexpectedly, considerable opposition to any formal definition of the expression "nonselfgoverning," and in the best tradition of diplomatic compromise, the Assembly adopted a resolution listing 74 nonselfgoverning territories in respect of which members had agreed to supply information.[2] The United Kingdom, as the resolution shows, had submitted or agreed to submit information concerning 41 territories including Northern Rhodesia (now Zambia) and Nyasaland (now Malawi) but not Southern Rhodesia.

From 1946 onward the evolution of the Rhodesian problem developed on two seemingly separate but actually interrelated levels—domestic and international—and although Britain consistently denied the legitimacy of the United Nations, discussions concerning Rhodesia could not remain entirely unaffected by them, and, indeed, it is fair to say that British policy was undoubtedly influenced by them, though to what degree it is difficult to ascertain.[3] As Geoffrey Goodwin has pointed out in his study on Britain and the United Nations, although "Britain from the start opposed the tendency to build up a counter part of the Trusteeship Council which would subject all colonies to the same scrutiny and criticism as the trust territories" by 1950, for political reasons, the British government had decided to "play as constructive and cooperative a part as possible" in the work of the Special Committee on Information, which had been set up by the General Assembly to receive and analyze the information transmitted under Article 73 of the Charter.[4] Britain, however, maintained its determination not to accept any implication of United Nations supervision, while the General Assembly, equally determined, asserted that it was for the United Nations to decide "whether any territory is or is not a territory whose people have not yet attained a full measure of self-government."[5]

Whatever the precise impact of the United Nations, it is clear that a certain parallelism begins to emerge in the 1950s between British policy toward Rhodesia and the General Assembly's actions.

In 1953, after a lengthy period of gestation, the Federation of Rhodesia and Nyasaland was formed. Under the federal constitution, each of the three constituent territories (Northern and Southern Rhodesia and Nyasaland) retained their political status: Northern Rhodesia and Nyasaland as protectorates and Southern Rhodesia as a self-governing colony. The federal government, however, was entrusted with responsibility for economic and financial affairs, defense, foreign affairs, transport and communications, immigration, and education. The Federation was a genuine attempt to create a multiracial society in central Africa, but it proved impossible to reconcile the aspirations of the African people for independence with the privileged position of the Europeans. The ultimate paradox of the system

15

was that the Parliament called upon to legislate for the two racial communities was completely dominated by a European minority representing a mere 3 percent of the total population of the Federation.

The General Assembly had not been idle, however, and by 1953 after several years of inquiry, study, and discussion, it had "gradually resolved by evolution through a series of resolutions the problem of whether the determination of the territories to which Chapter XI applies is a matter of domestic jurisdiction".[6] Not only did the Assembly make it clear that such determination was no longer an exclusively domestic prerogative, but in Resolution 742 (VIII) set out the factors that should be taken into account in deciding whether a particular territory had or had not attained a full measure of self-government.[7] Rhodesia did not meet many of the criteria of full self-government, particularly as regards suffrage.

The process of decolonization, which was nurtured by the General Assembly and which, as we have noted in another connection,[8] probably represents the United Nation's most important contribution to peaceful change in the post-1945 world, was not without its effect on the politics of the Federation. The increasing influence of African nationalist parties, especially in Northern Rhodesia and Nyasaland, and pressure at Westminister finally prevailed upon the British government to establish a commission under the chairmanship of Viscount Monckton to study the workings of the Federation and to advise on its future. The commission's report is the type of impartial document for which British democracy is justly renowned.[9] Its conclusions came as something of a shock to the Europeans in the Federation and undoubtedly surprised the Conservative government of the day. The commission stated flatly that the Federation could not be maintained in its present form and that no new form of association would succeed unless drastic changes were made in Rhodesia's racial policies. The commission recommended that the territories be granted the right to secede from the Federation regardless of the economic consequences.

The British government permitted Nyasaland to secede on December 19, 1962, and Northern Rhodesia on March 29, 1963. The formal dissolution of the Federation took effect on December 31, 1963. Northern Rhodesia and Nyasaland became independent states under majority rule on October 24 and July 6, 1964, respectively, Africanizing their names in the process to Zambia and Malawi. On December 1, 1964, they were both admitted to the United Nations.

With the imminent dissolution of the Federation already apparent, a constitutional conference was held in Salisbury in February 1961. For the first time in its history, a Prime Minister and African leaders of Rhodesia met to discuss the territory's future. The two principal African nationalist leaders in Rhodesia, Joshua Nkomo and Ndabaningi Sithole, participated in the conference but dismissed its final conclusions as unacceptable. A new Constitution to replace that of 1923 was,

16

however, approved by Rhodesian voters in a referendum and accepted by the United Kingdom Parliament.

Under the new Constitution, granted by Order in Council No. 2314 of December 6, 1961, few limitations were placed on the powers of the Rhodesian government. Rhodesia's constitutional position remained unaltered, that it to say, it continued to be a self-govering colony with executive authority vested in the governor as the Queen's representative. It was this 1961 Constitution that was in force at the time of the unilateral declaration of independence (UDI), and an examination of its provisions shows that very little progress, if any, had been made since 1923 toward the creation of a humane, civilized, multiracial society.

When the 1961 Constitution came into force, the British government surrendered the reserve powers it had held but never used under the 1923 Constitution. In place of the spurious reserve powers, a Declaration of Rights was written into the Constitution, and a constitutional council was established to examine new laws in order to ascertain whether they were compatible with the Declaration of Rights before receiving the assent of the governor. The constitutional council was completely ineffective, however, and it is doubtful whether it was ever seriously intended to function. The opinion of the constitutional council could be overruled by a two-thirds vote of the Assembly or (in most cases) after six months had elapsed following an objection. Furthermore, the council had no power to delay a money bill nor a bill certified by the Prime Minister to be urgent. The declared aim of the Declaration of Rights was to provide equal enjoyment of fundamental rights and freedoms for the individual, whatever his race, religion, place of origin, political opinions, color, or creed. But the very constitution into which the Declaration was written contained a provision which completely undermined the purpose of the Declaration. Under Section 70, paragraph 1(b), nothing done under a law in force immediately before the new Constitution became operative, and continuing in force, shall be held to be inconsistent with the Declaration. The Land Apportionment Act and the principal security laws, therefore, remained unaffected by the Declaration, which, deprived of any real force, could have no possible effect on the basic structure of racial discrimination already deeply embedded in Rhodesian society under existing legislation.

The franchise, as under the previous Constitution, was theoretically egalitarian, but in practice its qualifications discriminated against the Africans. Thus, for example, in a 65-member legislative assembly divided into 50 constituencies and 15 electoral districts, the overwhelming predominance of Europeans on the A-roll (electing

17

constituency members) guaranteed a minimum of 50 European members in the legislative assembly.*

NOTES

1. Ralph J. Bunche, "Trusteeship and Nonselfgoverning Territories in the Charter of the United Nations," Department of State, Bulletin, Vol. XIII, p. 1040.

2. Resolution 66 (I) concerning transmission of information under Article 73e of the Charter included the following: "The General Assembly notes that information has been transmitted by the Governments of Australia concerning conditions in Papua; France concerning conditions in French West Africa, French Equatorial Africa, French Somaliland, Madagascar and Dependencies, French Establishments in Oceania, Indo-China, French Establishments in India, New Caledonia and Dependencies, Saint Pierre et Miquelon, Morocco, Tunisia, the New Hebrides under Anglo-French Condominium, Martinique, Guadeloupe and Dependencies, French Guiana, and Reunion (without prejudice to the future status of these territories); New Zealand concerning conditions in the Cook Islands (without prejudice to any interpretation of the expression "Non-Self-Governing Territories" in view of the fact that the Cook Islands are an integral part of New Zealand); the United Kingdom concerning conditions in Barbados, Bermuda, British Guiana, British Honduras, Fiji, Gambia, Gibraltar, Leeward Islands, Mauritius, St. Lucia, and Zanzibar Protectorate; and the United States concerning conditions in Alaska, American Samoa, Guam, Hawaii, Panama Canal Zone, Puerto Rico and the Virgin Islands.

The General Assembly also notes that the following governments have declared their intention of transmitting information: Belgium on the Belgian Congo; Denmark on Greenland; the Netherlands on the Netherlands Indies, Surinam, and Curacao; New Zealand on the Tokelau Islands; and the United Kingdom on Aden (Colony and Protectorate), Bahamas, Basutoland, Bechuanaland Protectorate, British Somaliland Protectorate, Brunei, Cyprus, Dominica, Falkland Islands, Gold Coast (Colony and Protectorate), Grenada, Hong Kong, Jamaica, Kenya (Colony and Protectorate), Malayan Union, Malta, Nigeria, North Borneo, Northern Rhodesia, Nyasaland, St. Helena and Dependencies, St. Vincent, Sarawak, Seychelles, Sierra Leone, Singapore, Swaziland, Trinidad and Tobago, Uganda Protectorate, and the High Commission Territories of the Western Pacific (Gilbert and Ellice Islands Colony,

---

*In 1964, of the approximately 90,000 registered voters on the A-roll, 89,000 were Europeans.

British Solomon Islands Protectorate, Pitcairn Islands). See United Nations General Assembly Resolutions, First Session, 1946, p. 124.

3. A series of national studies on international organization was sponsored by the Carnegie Endowment in the 1950s. Among the questions addressed by each study was: What impact has the United Nations had on both the content and the conduct of national policy? Volumes published in this series included studies on Britain, Canada, the United States, Denmark, Greece, India, Israel, Sweden, and Switzerland.

4. Geoffrey L. Goodwin, Britain and the United Nations, Manhattan Publishing Co., New York, 1957, pp. 356-357.

5. United Nations General Assembly Resolution 334 (IV), December 2, 1949.

6. Rosalyn Higgins, The Development of International Law through the Political Organs of the United Nations, Oxford University Press, London, 1963, p. 112.

7. Resolution 742 (VIII): "Factors which should be taken into account in deciding whether a Territory is or is not a Territory whose people have not yet attained a full measure of self-government," is an extraordinary document and one which shows among other things how profound the influence of the General Assembly was. The Annex appended to the Resolution listed factors indicative of the attainment of independence, of other separate systems of self-government, and of free association. See United Nations General Assembly Resolutions, Seventh Session, 1953, p. 21.

8. Ralph Zacklin, The Amendment of the Constitutive Instruments of the United Nations and Specialized Agencies, A.W. Sijthoff, Leiden, 1968, pp. 188 ff.

9. "Report of the Advisory Commission on the Review of the Constitution of Rhodesia and Nyasaland," Cmnd. 1148, London, Her Majesty's Stationery Office, 1960.

CHAPTER

4

THE SEEDS
OF CONFLICT

Shortly after the promulgation of the 1961 Constitution, the General Assembly moved decisively on the issue of self-government in Rhodesia. The 1960 Declaration on the Granting of Independence to Colonial Countries and Peoples, Resolution 1514 (XV), which, as may be recalled, was adopted by the tumultuous Fifteenth Session of the General Assembly, had consolidated and reaffirmed the practice of the Assembly on this question. In its operative paragraphs, this landmark resolution declared:

1. The subjection of peoples to alien subjugation, domination, and exploitation constitutes a denial of fundamental human rights, is contrary to the Charter of the United Nations, and is an impediment to the promotion of world peace and cooperation.

2. All peoples have the right to self-determination; by virtue of that right they freely determine their political status and freely pursue their economic, social, and cultural development.

3. Inadequacy of political, economic, social, or educational preparedness should never serve as a pretext for delaying independence.

4. All armed action or repressive measures of all kinds directed against dependent peoples shall cease in order to enable them to exercise peacefully and freely their right to complete independence, and the integrity of their national territory shall be respected.

5. Immediate steps shall be taken, in trust and nonselfgoverning territories or all other territories that have not yet attained independence, to transfer all powers to the peoples of those territories, without any

conditions or reservations, in accordance with their freely expressed will and desire, without any distinction as to race, creed, or color, in order to enable them to enjoy complete independence and freedom.

6. Any attempt aimed at the partial or total disruption of the national unity and the territorial integrity of a country is incompatible with the purposes and principles of the Charter of the United Nations.

7. All states shall observe faithfully and strictly the provisions of the Charter of the United Nations, the Universal Declaration of Human Rights, and the present Declaration on the basis of equality, noninterference in the internal affairs of all states, and respect for the sovereign rights of all peoples and their territorial integrity.[1]

In March 1962, the Special Committee of Seventeen, which had been established to examine progress in the implementation of the Declaration, decided to consider whether Rhodesia was in fact self-governing. The General Assembly resolution, in virtue of which the Special Committee was acting, stated that it "was mindful of the fact that the indigenous inhabitants [of Rhodesia] have not been adequately represented in the legislature and not represented at all in the government."[2] Over the objections of the United Kingdom for whom the Special Committee's action was ultra vires,[3] the Special Committee endorsed the finding of its subcommittee that Southern Rhodesia had not attained self-government, a finding that was unequivocally confirmed by the General Assembly itself in Resolution 1747 (XVI). Basing itself on the opinion that "the vast majority of the people of Southern Rhodesia have rejected the Constitution of December 6, 1961" and finding a "denial of equal political rights and liberties to the vast majority of the people of Southern Rhodesia," the Assembly affirmed that Rhodesia was a nonselfgoverning territory within the meaning of Chapter XI of the Charter and requested the Administering Authority:

(a) to [convene] a constitutional conference, in which there shall be full participation of representatives of all political parties, for the purpose of formulating a constitution for Southern Rhodesia, in place of the Constitution of December 6, 1961, which would ensure the rights of the majority of the people, on the basis of "one man, one vote," in conformity with the principles of the Charter of the United Nations and the Declaration on the Granting of Independence to Colonial Countries and

Peoples, embodied in General Assembly Resolution 1514 (XV);
(b) to take immediate steps to restore all rights of the non-European population and remove all restraints and restrictions in law and in practice . . . based on racial discrimination;
(c) to grant amnesty to, and ensure the immediate release of, all political prisoners.[4]

Resolution 1747 (XVI) represented a watershed in the relations between the General Assembly and the United Kingdom with regard to Rhodesia. The evolution of international public policy with respect to the principle of self-determination, culminating in the Declaration on the Granting of Independence to Colonial Countries and Peoples, and its subsequent application to Southern Rhodesia constituted a clear and unequivocal statement by one of the highest organs of the international community, the General Assembly, of the foundations and principles of the right to self-determination which, in its view, should govern the devolution of Rhodesia to independent status.

The addressee of this statement, a permanent member of the Security Council, while not out of sympathy with the general statement of principles embodied in the Declaration, nevertheless considered its application to Rhodesia inappropriate on the grounds that the territory in question had been self-governing since 1923 and considered the action of the Special Committee and its subcommittee ultra vires. For this reason, in the view of this member, General Assembly Resolution 1747 (XVI) itself was tainted.

A clearer case of confrontation and interaction between international and national jurisdiction would be difficult to find. It is appropriate, therefore, at this juncture to examine the content of the rule of international public policy affirmed by the Assembly and its legal nature. Before doing so, however, a brief summary of the evolution of Britain's colonial policy and its posture in the United Nations at this juncture may be helpful.

The evolution of Britain's colonial policy between 1945 and 1965 must rank, without question, as one of the most pragmatic, enlightened, and intelligent exercises of power by any major state in modern times. While France became mired in futile and savage wars in Indo-China and Algeria, while Belgium demonstrated in the Congo a precipitousness bordering on the criminal, while Portugal obstinately and senselessly clung to Angola and Mozambique, and while South Africa openly defied the United Nations on South West Africa, Britain, after the "emergencies" in Malaya and Kenya, moved with all deliberate speed to the orderly transfer of power in its colonies on the basis of majority rule.

In retrospect, the speed and harmony with which this was performed were quite extraordinary. It demonstrated both a pragmatic flexibility in the conduct of British policy and an attachment to fundamental values of the kind embodied in the principle of self-determination: Policy and principle were here combined to a quite exceptional degree. Rhodesia thus emerges as an anomaly, contrapuntal to the main theme of British colonial policy.

During the wartime evolution of the United Nations, Britain had strongly resisted American and Soviet attempts to write into the Charter an international administration for all colonies.[5] This position, however, did not preclude it from supporting the positive obligations of administering powers "to promote the political, economic, social, and educational advancement of the inhabitants of the trust territories and their progressive development toward self-government or independence," as expressed in Article 76 of the Charter. It may be assumed, therefore, that this position would apply a fortiori to Britain's nontrust territories. Churchill's celebrated dictum notwithstanding—"I did not become His Majesty's Prime Minister in order to preside over the dissolution of the British Empire"—beginning with Ghana's independence in 1957, Britain in the space of a few short years virtually completed the process of devolution of its sovereignty in Africa. The classic statement of Britain's position in this regard and its moral foundations are contained in the celebrated "wind of change" speech delivered by Prime Minister Macmillan to a joint assembly of the two Houses of the South African Parliament in 1960.

> Nothing we do in this small world can be done in a corner
> or remain hidden . . . it has been our aim, in countries
> for which we have borne responsibility, not only to raise
> the material standards of living, but to create a society
> which respects the rights of individuals—a society in
> which men are given the opportunity to grow to their full
> stature, and that must in our view include the opportunity
> to have an increasing share in political power and re-
> sponsibility; a society in which individual merit, and
> individual merit alone, is the criterion for man's advance-
> ment whether political or economic . . . in countries in-
> habited by several different races, it has been our aim
> to find the means by which the community can become
> more of a community, and fellowship can be fostered
> between its various parts. . . . It is our earnest desire
> to give South Africa our support and encouragement,
> but . . . there are some aspects of your policies which
> make it impossible for us to do this without being false

to our own deep convictions about the political destinies
of free men, to which in our own territories we are trying
to give effect.

We have cited this speech at some length because it illuminates two
of the major themes of this study. The first is the indivisibility of
the modern world ("Nothing we can do in this small world can be
done in a corner or remain hidden . . .") and its connotations with
respect to the international and national jurisdiction relationship.
The second is the articulation of fundamental values (the right of
self-determination) on a national level that mirror or are mirrored
by analogous statements on the international plane. Macmillan's
speech preceded the Declaration on the Granting of Independence to
Colonial Countries and Peoples by almost a full year, but in essence
the two statements are remarkably similar.

Thus, ironically enough, Britain, which more than any other
colonial power was in harmony with the prevailing United Nations
doctrine on self-determination and which had brought about a massive
transformation of African territories to independent statehood, found
itself arraigned before the bar of world public opinion with respect
to a territory which, from the point of view of British constitutional
law, had been self-governing for almost 40 years. The cumulative
effect of General Assembly Resolutions 1514 (XV) and 1747 (XVI)
could not be lightly dismissed, however. In the opinion of the General
Assembly, Rhodesia was not self-governing, as a consequence of which,
presumably, certain effects ensued.

The precise legal nature and effect of resolutions adopted by
the United Nations General Assembly have been a source of considerable doctrinal controversy for over 25 years. This is not the
place to enter into a detailed examination of the complex phenomenon
of international resolutions;[6] suffice it to say that in that small part
of the field of international law with which we are concerned, resolutions have clearly effected a revolution in the relationship between
the international community and sovereign states. As Jorge Castaneda
points out,

> . . . resolutions, practices, and mechanisms for the pro-
> tection of dependent peoples, which have been developed
> by the United Nations through the years with a progres-
> sively diminishing direct basis in the Charter, have had
> the combined effect of modifying the entire chapter of
> international law pertaining to territorial sovereignty.[7]

For Castaneda, whose recent study represents one of the rare inductive analyses of UN Resolutions, ". . . some resolutions of international bodies can be manifestations and means of externalization of

international legal norms, that is to say, formal sources of international law."[8] Castaneda identifies six categories of "nonrecommendatory" resolutions which, in his view, are capable of producing "true juridical effects against which members have no legal recause":[9]

1. resolutions pertaining to the structure and operation of the United Nations;
2. certain resolutions concerning international peace and security;
3. resolutions that determine the existence of facts or concrete legal situations;
4. resolutions whose binding force rests on instruments other than the Charter;
5. resolutions that express and register agreement among the members of an organ; and
6. resolutions that contain declarations or other pronouncements of a general nature.

The essential trait of declaratory resolutions, in Castaneda's view, "is that they do not create law, but that they recognize and declare it."[10] While recognizing that the basic foundation for the binding force of rules or principles "declared" by a resolution resides in the fact that they are already, or may be considered to be, customary rules or general principles of law, Castaneda agrees with Jessup that the declaratory resolution as such has a fully probative legal value—in other words, the resolution is "persuasive evidence of the existence of the rule of law" which it enunciates.[11] Thus

> The recognition and formal expression of a customary rule or a general principle of law by the General Assembly constitutes a juris et de jure presumption that such a rule or principle is a part of positive international law, that is to say, a legal assumption or fiction that does not allow proof to the contrary, and in the face of which an opposing individual position therefore lacks legal efficacy.[12]

The legal value of any particular declaratory resolution then will depend on the degree to which it may be said to reflect customary law or general principles of law—an evaluation of considerable difficulty under the most propitious circumstances and doubly so in the context of self-determination. The Declaration on Granting of Independence to Colonial Countries and Peoples would, on the face of it, appear to express both an ideal and a specific legal obligation which renders it difficult to characterize. The Declaration, in Castaneda's words, " . . . symbolizes and concretizes a new politico-juridical conception: the definite repudiation and end of colonialism."[13]

The Declaration must, therefore, probably be viewed as a mechanism compensating for the inability of the contemporary international society to establish an effective institutionalized and permanent legislative organ. The General Assembly lacks such formal authority to legislate, but through an evolution of its functions and powers and its interpretation of the Charter, it has, in the specific field of colonialism and self-determination at any rate, assumed a de facto authority to articulate the existence of certain principles which, based on Charter provisions and representing the quasi-unanimous opinion of the members of the international community, create general legal effects inherent in international public policy.

Resolution 1747 (XVI), on the other hand, is subordinate to the Declaration and may be characterized as a resolution that purports to determine the existence of a concrete legal situation and expresses or registers agreement among members of a particular organ. The determination in Resolution 1747 (XVI) is "that the territory of Southern Rhodesia is nonselfgoverning territory within the meaning of Chapter XI of the Charter" as a consequence of which the United Kingdom is "requested" to undertake certain measures. While it would be an exaggeration to say that Resolution 1747 (XVI) posits a legal obligation on the part of the addressee, it does constitute a pronouncement of the organization, and the question therefore arises as to what legal value, if any, should be ascribed to it.

In this connection, it is probably relevant to note that on a roll-call vote, only one member state (South Africa) voted against the Resolution. The high number of abstentions (27) may also be significant in that they represent acquiescence in, if not actual approval of, the Resolution. The United Kingdom was present but did not vote. At the very least, therefore, Resolution 1747 (XVI) is representative of the opinion of a principal organ of the United Nations with regard to a particular factual and legal situation and as such has legal validity. In other words, measures taken by the addressee in pursuance of the Resolution would have been lawful measures.

It follows, therefore, that the importance of Resolution 1747 (XVI) when read in conjunction with Resolution 1514 (XV) stems from the fact that it is a statement by the international community's most representative organ of the moral and legal basis for intervention by the administering authority. Had the United Kingdom government been prepared to exercise its lawful authority in Rhodesia, in support of the principles it professed to uphold, it would have received the virtually unanimous support of the international community. Resolution 1747 (XVI) was in fact a mandate for intervention issued by the General Assembly on behalf of the United Nations. Unfortunately, instead of the decisiveness and determination which might have been expected with such a mandate, the respective governments (Conservative and Labor) exhibited varying degrees of ambivalence, ambiguity, and, finally, abject resignation in their confrontation with the white minority represented by the Rhodesian Front Party.

By 1962, with a combination of vocal Afro-Asian demands in the United Nations, white minority neurosis in Rhodesia, and endless vacillation on the part of the British government, the Rhodesian problem was rapidly becoming a full-scale crisis which was to culminate in the fatal and, given the supine nature of government policy, inevitable unilateral declaration of independence (UDI) in 1965.

NOTES

1. See United Nations General Assembly Resolutions, 1960, Vol. I, pp. 66-67.

2. Resolution 1745 (XVI). See United Nations General Assembly Resolutions, Sixteenth Session, Vol. I, p. 44.

3. See Rosalyn Higgins, The Development of International Law through the Political Organs of the United Nations, Oxford University Press, London, 1963, p. 113.

4. Resolution 1747 (XVI). See United Nations General Assembly Resolutions, Sixteenth Session, Vol. II, p. 3.

5. Goodwin, op. cit., p. 348.

6. We may indicate the following writings from an abundant literature as being particularly interesting: Clive Parry, The Sources and Evidences of International Law, Manchester University Press, 1965; F. Blaine Sloan, "The Binding Force of a 'Recommendation' of the General Assembly of the United Nations," British Yearbook of International Law, Vol. XXV, pp. 1-33, 1948; D. H. N. Johnson, "The Effect of Resolutions of the General Assembly of the United Nations," British Yearbook of International Law, Vol. XXXII, pp. 97-123, 1955-56; and Michel Virally, "La Valeur juridique des recommendations des organisations internationales," Annuaire francais de droit international, pp. 66-97, 1956.

7. Jorge Castaneda, Legal Effects of United Nations Resolutions, Columbia University Press, New York, 1969, pp. 3-4.

8. Ibid., p. 5.

9. Ibid., p. vii.

10. Ibid., p. 168.

11. Philip C. Jessup, A Modern Law of Nations, New York, 1948, p. 46.

12. Castaneda, op. cit., p. 172.

13. Ibid., p. 175.

CHAPTER

5

TOWARD
THE ABYSS

The drama that unfolded in Salisbury, London, and New York benefited, like all such crises, from a cast of characters which, if they had not existed, would almost certainly have had to be invented. The dramatis personae of the Rhodesian drama in the period 1962 to 1965 included farmers and tobacco growers who were part-time politicians, a Soviet sinologist functioning as the USSR's permanent representative at the United Nations, an Earl who had emerged from secret conclaves of the Conservative Party to become Prime Minister of Britain, two rival African nationalist leaders both of whom during the relevant period were at various times imprisoned or banished, sundry politicians and diplomats one of whom held center stage in two separate incarnations. Not a few of these figures possessed an instinctive sense of the dramatic so that the theatrical simile is not entirely inappropriate.

If the plot contained its fair share of dramatic incident, the dialogue with its constant accusations and rebuttals tended to be somewhat repetitive. Through it all, however, the main actors consorted in a dialogue of the deaf so that the best efforts of multilateral and bilateral diplomacy were ultimately unavailing.

As 1962 began, there were signs, misleading as they turned out, of a more flexible attitude on the part of the governing minority in Rhodesia. In January 1962 an amendment to the Rhodesian Electoral Act took effect, which resulted in an increase in African suffrage, and at the end of January Prime Minister Whitehead announced that the government planned to repeal the discriminatory provisions of the Land Apportionment Act. These measures were doubtless an attempt to moderate the extremist settler position, but inasmuch as they were also intended to mollify the United Nations, and especially the Afro-Asian group in the General Assembly, the maneuver was unsuccessful. Resolution 1747 (XVI) had been adopted by the General

Assembly in June 1962 against a background of mounting violence and repression in Rhodesia. In October 1962, Sir Hugh Foot, Britain's Permanent Representative to the United Nations Trusteeship Council and the man chiefly responsible for defending the British position at the United Nations, resigned in protest over British government policy on Rhodesia. Foot had defended Britain's policy of nonintervention and took the view that in adopting Resolution 1747 (XVI) the General Assembly had acted ultra vires since Rhodesia had been a self-governing colony since 1923. However, in his view this did not absolve the United Kingdom government from its duty toward the African majority in Rhodesia, and indeed by the summer of 1962 he had come to the conclusion that if no new initiatives were forthcoming from London, he would be unable to continue as the government spokesman on Rhodesia. Commenting some time later on the consequences of Resolution 1747 (XVI), he stated:

> Certainly, I did not feel that we would be justified in taking no action at all. We needed some time to maneuver, to find a way to avoid the approaching dangers, not merely to procrastinate and drift. I could not imagine that the British Government intended to do nothing about Southern Rhodesia, and that the resolution calling for a conference was to be altogether ignored.[1]

In London for consultations following the General Assembly vote, Sir Hugh Foot urged specific actions on the government:

> I recommended that the Southern Rhodesian Government should be pressed to do three things—to release the very few Africans then under restrictions, to withhold the new repressive legislation then being prepared, and to grant at least some relaxation in the restrictions on the African franchise. . . . My recommendation was that the British Government should state at once that after the elections a conference of all concerned, including of course the Africans, would be called, and that it should also be clearly stated that no change in the constitutional status of Southern Rhodesia would be approved by the British Government until a new course had been worked out and agreed at such a full conference. I maintained, and still strongly maintain, that such action was fully within the competence of the British Government. There was nothing to prevent the British Government stating its intention to call a full conference . . . and there was equally nothing to prevent the British Government making it quite

clear, as indeed it apparently has since done, that independence will not be granted to Southern Rhodesia on the basis of continued white domination.[2]

The resignation of an ambassador to the United Nations would not normally create more than a ripple on the waters of multilateral diplomacy, but Sir Hugh Foot was no ordinary ambassador. Although he himself both at the time and since has tended to downplay the importance of his act of resignation, there can be no doubt that in the context of the time and having regard to his distinguished record in the Colonial Service and the respect and esteem with which he was regarded by United Nations delegations, his resignation externalized a polarization of opinion within the British administration on how to approach the problem of Rhodesia.

The resignation certainly alarmed the Rhodesian government, possibly fearing a hardening in the British position, but the British government quickly dissipated any uncertainty as to its intentions by announcing that it would not change its policy of nonintervention in Rhodesian affairs. Prime Minister Whitehead meanwhile pledged to end racial discrimination and even went so far as to suggest the possibility of African control of the Rhodesian government in 15 years, a prediction which almost certainly hastened his downfall since, in the December elections, the right wing Rhodesian Front Party virtually obliterated Whitehead's United Federal Party.

The dissolution of the Federation of Rhodesia and Nyasaland, which took effect on December 31, 1963, was a mixed blessing for the British government. On the one hand, it paved the way for complete independence of both Zambia and Malawi; on the other hand, it posed the acute problem of how to dispose of the air and ground forces of the Federation. Despite the fact that the General Assembly had already characterized the Rhodesian situation as a threat to international peace and security and although it might seem even to the uninitiated that the transfer of air and ground forces to Rhodesia could only improve its military position, the British government proposed to transfer the bulk of these forces to Rhodesia, making it the second most powerful military force in Africa. A Security Council resolution calling on Britain not to transfer these forces to Rhodesia was vetoed by Britain in September 1963.

With Zambia and Malawi both attaining independence in 1964, the pressures for Rhodesian independence increased. In April 1964 the Rhodesian Front leader Winston Field was forced to resign under pressure from the right wing of his party and was succeeded as Prime Minister by Ian Smith. The new government's first official action was to banish Joshua Nkomo, the President of Zimbabwe African Peoples Union (ZAPU), and three of his aides to a remote part of the country for one year.

In September 1964 Ian Smith conferred in London with British Prime Minister Alec Douglas Home, who pledged independence for Rhodesia on condition that a majority of both blacks and whites declared themselves in favor of it. Since by this time the Reverend Sithole, leader of the ZANU, had also been imprisoned, the likelihood of Ian Smith receiving the support of the majority of Africans in Rhodesia might have appeared somewhat slim. Smith, however, was confident of receiving African support, which he proposed to demonstrate by polling the views of 800 government subsidized chiefs and headmen, a maneuver which even the Conservative government was unlikely to accept. In October 1964, however, the Labor Party returned to power after 13 years in opposition. The resulting shift in relations between London and Salisbury, superficially at any rate, should have resulted in a more uncompromising policy on the part of the British government. British policy in central Africa had, for several years, been one of the few real issues between the Conservative and Labor Parties. The Conservatives in office had been somewhat suspect on the question of Rhodesia because of personal and corporate links with the white minority, whereas the Labor Party in opposition had consistently resisted all attempts to short-change the African majority.

If nothing else, the advent of Harold Wilson certainly produced an escalation of language. In a declaration published on October 27, 1964, he warned Rhodesia that "a unilateral declaration of independence would be an open act of defiance and rebellion and it would be treasonable to take steps to give effect to it," adding that such an attempt would meet with the direst consequences.

The warning passed unheeded. On November 5, 1964, in a referendum organized by the government in Salisbury, 90 percent of those voting were in favor of independence under the 1961 Constitution. Only 60 percent of the registered voters took part in the referendum, however.

Further contacts were sought by the British government with the Rhodesians at the beginning of 1965. In February the Commonwealth Relations Secretary and the Lord Chancellor met with members of the Rhodesian government and African leaders, including Joshua Nkomo and the Reverend Sithole. The latter insisted on the installation of majority government before accession to independence.

In April, following the publication of a white book by the Salisbury regime, Prime Minister Wilson, speaking in the House of Commons, issued a solemn warning that only negotiation and respect for the law would bring Rhodesia independence, adding that an illegal declaration of independence would be considered by his government as "an act of rebellion" that would deprive the colony of British economic aid and preferential tariffs. This was the first allusion to the possibility of applying sanctions against Rhodesia.

The fourteenth Commonwealth Prime Ministers Conference was held in London in June 1965. The key issue, and one on which the future of the Commonwealth hinged, was Rhodesia. The African leaders, in particular Julius Nyerere of Tanzania, proposed that the British government should convoke a constitutional conference within three months to be attended by all of Rhodesia's political leaders. Should the regime in Salisbury refuse to participate in such a conference, the British should suspend the 1961 Constitution and appoint a provisional government with a view to preparing Rhodesia's independence on a basis acceptable to the population as a whole. The final communique of the Conference represented a compromise between the British and African positions. Both points of view were set out, and while Britain conceded that a constitutional conference would, at the appropriate time, be a natural step, it was unable to accept the African demand for an immediate conference, preferring to pursue its negotiations with the Salisbury regime.[3]

On another front the British government was defending its policies in the United Nations Security Council. There, Sir Hugh Foot had reappeared as Lord Caradon, having been elevated to the peerage by Harold Wilson and appointed Minister of State for Foreign Affairs and Permanent Representative to the United Nations, where he now had to withstand the attacks of spokesmen of the Organization of African Unity and the personal attacks of the Soviet Union's Nicolai Federenko who, not content with attacking British policy, also accused Lord Caradon of having changed his views on becoming a peer, using as his chief weapon ample citations from A Start in Freedom, which had been published in 1964.

The Salisbury government reacted with equal derision to the demands of the United Nations, the Commonwealth Prime Ministers Conference, and the threats of the British government. In August 1964 Ian Smith reaffirmed publicly that Rhodesia could declare its independence without exposing itself to any danger, internal or external, adding in an excess of optimism, as it turns out, that it would obtain official recognition from several countries.[4] In September the Salisbury regime nominated a diplomatic representative to Lisbon, a calculated challenge to the British government which, under the 1961 Constitution, retained responsibility for the diplomatic-consular relations of Rhodesia.

After fruitless Smith-Wilson talks in London from October 4 to October 8, 1965 and in an eleventh-hour attempt to find a way out of the impasse of British-Rhodesian relations, Prime Minister Wilson flew to Salisbury at the end of October. In the meantime, on October 12 the General Assembly of the United Nations by a vote of 107 to 2, with one abstention, had requested the British government to take "all possible measures" to prevent a unilateral declaration of independence by the white Rhodesian minority.[5] In Salisbury Prime Minister Wilson proposed the establishment of a Royal Commission to inquire into the possibility of reaching a negotiated independence and the acceptance of such independence by the African majority on the basis of the 1961 Constitution. This proposal was rejected by Smith on November 3, and on November 5 the Salisbury government proclaimed a state of emergency for three months. On the same day, by a vote of 82 to 9, with 18 abstentions, the General Assembly requested Britain "to employ all necessary measures, including military force" to prevent a unilateral declaration of independence.[6] After having refused a last offer to meet with Wilson in Malta, Smith proclaimed the independence of Rhodesia on November 11, 1965.

World and British reaction was swift. The United Nations General Assembly promptly adopted a resolution calling on Britain to take all necessary steps to end the rebellion,[7] and in a speech to the British public on November 11, 1965 Wilson condemned the unilateral declaration of independence as "an illegal act and one ineffective in law."[8] There immediately followed a series of decisions by the British government, including the dismissal of the Prime Minister and other ministers of the Rhodesian government, the recall of the British High Commissioner in Rhodesia, the expulsion of the Rhodesian High Commissioner in London, the cessation of the export of arms to Rhodesia and of British aid, exclusion of Rhodesia from the sterling area, a series of monetary, financial, and economic measures, refusal to recognize passports delivered or renewed by the Rhodesian authorities, an obligation for the members of the Rhodesian armed forces and police not to take up arms in favor of the Rhodesian government, not to do anything that might help maintain its illegality, and a prohibition on Rhodesian civil servants from carrying out any work that might aid the Rhodesian government in its rebellion. All these sanctionary measures were the object of appropriate British legislation. At the time informed opinion believed that these measures, together with the cooperation that could be expected from the members of the United Nations, would strangle the Rhodesian economy within a matter of months. Notwithstanding Britain's avowed refusal to the use of force to suppress the rebellion, the confrontation between a small white minority numbering little more than 200,000 and the rest of the world was expected to be short and swift.

NOTES

1. Sir Hugh Foot, A Start in Freedom, Harper and Row, New York, 1964, p. 218.
2. Ibid., p. 219.

3. Harold Wilson, <u>A Personal Record: The Labour Government, 1964-1970</u>, Little, Brown, Boston, 1971, pp. 118-119.
4. <u>Le Monde</u>, August 10, 1965.
5. General Assembly Resolution 2012 (XX).
6. General Assembly Resolution 2022 (XX).
7. General Assembly Resolution 2024 (XX).
8. <u>The Times</u> (London), November 13, 1965.

As the late Hans Kelsen observed, the separation of law from politics is possible insofar as law is not an end in itself but a specific social technique for the achievement of ends determined by politics.1 Kelsen's monumental work of critical analysis of the Charter of the United Nations was strongly motivated by the recognition that legal norms formulated in words frequently have more than one meaning, which is the reason why every legal instrument has its own life:

> That the law is open to more than one interpretation is
> certainly detrimental to legal security; but it has the
> advantage of making the law adaptable to changing cir-
> cumstances, without the requirement of formal alter-
> ation.2

The Kelsenian view of the relationship of law to politics, particu-larly in the context of the Charter, has a distinctly prescient quality, for as we know today the Charter has proved to be surprisingly elastic. Although provided with elaborate formal procedures for amendment and revision, formal amendments to the Charter have been extremely rare, while revision, though frequently evoked, has predictably been shunned.3 On the other hand, a number of informal or de facto modi-fications significantly affecting the relationship of the two principal organs—the General Assembly and Security Council—have evolved. through interpretation of the Charter.4

The constitutional and organic tensions, which produce these so-called de facto modifications, have been particularly acute in two main areas of United Nations activity: collective security (in particu-lar, the voting procedures of the Security Council and the expansion of the General Assembly's powers with regard to the maintenance of international peace and security) and decolonization. The especial significance of Rhodesia, in this context, is that it links these two areas of great political sensitivity. Rhodesia has been, and continues to be, an important element both in the de facto modification of Charter provisions concerning decolonization, particularly with regard to the development of the General Assembly's role in the granting of independence to colonial countries and people, and in the interpretation and implementation of the collective measures provisions of Chapter VII of the Charter. Indeed, the development of the General Assembly's role on granting of independence, as it gradually came to be focused on Rhodesia, was fundamental to the ultimate legal-constitutional basis of sanctions and provided an important legitimizing link between the General Assembly and the Security Council without which it may not have been possible to institute sanctions at all.

From the perspective, therefore, of international law and international institutions, or that amalgam of the two sometimes referred to as international constitutional law, an important function of the policy of sanctions, in addition to the political goal of inducing change within Rhodesia in conformity with the international community's expectations, is their probative evaluation of the Charter system as a social technique for the achievement of political ends.

THE SECURITY COUNCIL

Article 24, paragraph 1, of the Charter confers "primary responsibility for the maintenance of international peace and security" on the Security Council. The Council is deemed to exercise this responsibility on behalf of all the members of the organization who are under an obligation to accept and to carry out the Council's decisions.

With regard to pacific settlement of disputes (Chapter VI of the Charter), the Council may adopt only nonbinding recommendations, but "threats to the peace, breaches of the peace, and acts of aggression" are subject to the provisions of Chapter VII of the Charter under which the Security Council exercises legally binding authority vis-à-vis all member states.

When the nature or characteristics of any particular dispute or situation call for action on the part of the United Nations, the first task of the Security Council is to make a determination under Article 39 as to "the existence of any threat to the peace, breach of the peace, or act of aggression." The Charter does not define these terms, and the Security Council is free, therefore, to make its determination on the basis of whatever factual and other considerations it considers appropriate.[5] Should the Security Council arrive at an Article 39 determination, it may proceed to initiate a variety of measures under the terms of Articles 39, 40, 41, and 42 of the Charter: It may "call upon the parties concerned to comply with such provisional measures as it deems necessary or desirable" (Article 40); it may make recommendations (Article 39); it may employ measures not involving the use of armed force (Article 41); or it may use force (Article 42).

The Security Council has frequently invoked the provisional measures procedure, calling upon the parties to a dispute to cease fighting,[6] to refrain from importing war materials into a certain zone,[7] or in calling for withdrawal of troops from foreign territory.[8] In addition, Security Council recommendations under Article 39 have been the basis for, among other things, the military action by individual members in Korea[9] and the peace-keeping operation in Cyprus.[10] The measures not involving the use of armed force outlined in Article 41 "may include complete or partial interruption of economic relations and of rail, sea, air, coastal, telegraphic, radio and other means of communication, and the severance of diplomatic relations." These measures have only rarely been invoked. In 1963 the Security Council called upon all states "to cease forthwith the sale and shipment of arms, ammunition of all types and military vehicles" to the Republic of South Africa[11] and to end the sale and shipment of equipment and materials for making and maintaining arms and ammunition in South Africa,[12] and in 1965, the Security Council called for a break in economic relations with Southern Rhodesia including an embargo on oil and petroleum products.[13] These Resolutions, however, were not mandatory decisions of the Council and, as we shall see below, it was not until 1966 that the first mandatory sanctions under Articles 39 and 41 of the Charter were adopted.

The fourth course of action open to the Security Council is the use of force. If it concludes that nonmilitary enforcement measures under Article 41 "would be inadequate or have proved to be inadequate," the Council may under Article 42 "take such action by air, sea, or land forces as may be necessary to maintain or restore international peace and security." The implementation of Article 42, however, is contingent upon agreements to be concluded under Article 43, paragraph 2:

> Such agreement or agreements shall govern the numbers
> and types of forces, their degree of readiness and general location, and the nature of the facilities and assistance to be provided.

An obligation on the part of a member state to give the United Nations military assistance may only arise, therefore, under a specific agreement, and since for political reasons no such agreements have been concluded, the United Nations is effectively incapacitated from the possibility of applying the military sanctions provided for in Articles 42 to 47 of the Charter. These provisions have remained unfulfilled and represent a reverse or negative de facto modification of the Charter inasmuch as the practice of states has resulted in a dimunition rather than an expansion of the functions and powers of the organization.

THE GENERAL ASSEMBLY

In contradistinction to the relative inactivity of the Security Council, however, we must balance the development of the General Assembly's role in the maintenance of international peace and security. Although under Article 10 of the Charter the General Assembly has wide powers of recommendation on "any questions or any matters within the scope of the present Charter or relating to the powers and functions of any organs provided for in the present Charter" comprising in particular "any questions relating to the maintenance of international peace and security" (Article 11, paragraph 2), these recommendatory powers are nonbinding, and the scheme of the Charter quite clearly imposes on the Security Council primary responsibility in this field. The question is whether the General Assembly has a secondary responsibility should the Security Council fail for any reason to exercise its primary responsibility? According to one point of view, the Security Council's jurisdiction under Chapter VII is exclusive and cannot be exercised by the General Assembly acting as a substitute.* A second interpretation, however, contends that the Charter does not eliminate a subsidiary responsibility which must devolve upon the General Assembly when the Security Council fails to act.† This latter interpretation found expression in the Uniting for Peace Resolution of November 3, 1950, where the General Assembly interpreted its powers as follows:

> If the Security Council, because of lack of unanimity of the Permanent Members, fails to exercise its primary responsibility for the maintenance of international peace

---

*This strict construction of the Security Council's jurisdiction and its relationship to the General Assembly is identified with the Soviet Union. However, in the Suez affair of 1956 and the Middle East crisis of 1958, the Soviet Union appeared to find exceptions to the application of this interpretation.

†This point of view has the support of the Latin American, African, and Asian members.

and security in any case where there appears to be a
threat to peace, breach of the peace or act of aggression,
the General Assembly shall consider the matter immediately with a view to making appropriate recommendations to Members for collective measures, including in the case of a breach of the peace or act of
aggression the use of armed force when necessary, to
maintain or restore international peace and security.
If not in session at the time, the General Assembly may
meet in an emergency special session within 24 hours of
the request thereof. Such an emergency special session
shall be called if requested by the Security Council on the
vote of any seven members, or by a majority of the
members of the United Nations.[14]

The General Assembly has invoked its secondary responsibility under
the terms of the Uniting for Peace Resolution on several occasions,
taking care, however, to circumscribe such activities to peace-keeping operations, avoiding enforcement action as such. The General
Assembly has, however, recommended nonmilitary measures on
several occasions. In 1962 it requested members to break off diplomatic relations with the government of the Republic of South Africa,[15]
and in 1965 it urged similar measures with regard to Portugal,[16] the
former because of the racial (apartheid) policies of South Africa and
the latter because of the repression and military operations carried
out in the Portuguese colonies in Africa. The General Assembly
has also recommended embargoes on arms and war materials to be
applied to Albania and Bulgaria in connection with the civil war in
Greece in 1948,[17] to North Korea and the People's Republic of China
in connection with the Korean War in 1951,[18] to Portugal in connection with her colonial policies in 1962,[19] and to South Africa in connection with the mandated territory of South West Africa in 1963.[20]

    A somewhat similar enlargement of the General Assembly's
powers has taken place with respect to decolonization. By 1962, when
the Rhodesian problem first came to the attention of the General
Assembly, the Assembly had already significantly expanded its role
in the granting of independence to colonial countries and peoples
beyond the rather anodyne functions and powers outlined in Chapter
XI of the Charter, in which the obligations of the administering states
are cast in the most general terms. The only concrete obligation to
emerge from the San Francisco Conference was an undertaking by
the administering members "to transmit regularly to the Secretary-
General for information purposes, subject to such limitation as
security and constitutional considerations may require, statistical
and other information of a technical nature relating to economic,

social, and educational conditions in the territories for which they are respectively responsible . . ." [Article 73, paragraph (e)]. Article 73 does not expressly confer on any organ of the United Nations, principal or subsidiary, a supervisory power or function with regard to nonselfgoverning territories. Through its interpretation of Article 73, however, the General Assembly succeeded in "modifying" the Charter in two important respects. Firstly, it established its competence to examine the information transmitted by the administering members, which under a strict interpretation of Article 73, paragraph (e), was to be submitted to the Secretary-General for information purposes only, and, secondly, it broadened the nature of the information to be transmitted, to embrace political information as well as the statistical and technical information referred to in Article 73, paragraph (e), and determined the form in which the information should be submitted.[21]

This evolution of the General Assembly's functions and powers in respect of Chapter XI was, of course, a necessary and essential prelude to the General Assembly's involvement with the Rhodesian problem. By establishing that it had the competence to determine whether a particular territory is nonselfgoverning within the terms of Chapter XI of the Charter and, accordingly, that it was competent to lay down the criteria upon which such a determination could be based, the Assembly in effect created the legal and constitutional basis for its intervention in the Rhodesian affair in 1962. Since 1962, of course, the situation in Rhodesia has been under virtually constant scrutiny by the General Assembly and the Security Council, and although, constitutionally, the Council alone disposes of the power to impose mandatory decisions on member states, it is the Assembly that has served as the watchdog of the international community and that has provided the real impetus for the Council's actions.

Finally, a discussion of the role of the General Assembly would be incomplete without a reference to the important role played by the Special Committee on Decolonization. Article 22 of the Charter confers upon the General Assembly the power to establish "such subsidiary organs as it deems necessary for the performance of its functions." Following the adoption by the General Assembly of the Declaration on the Granting of Independence to Colonial Countries and Peoples [Resolution 1514 (XV)], the Assembly established the Special Committee on Decolonization.[22] The terms of reference of the Committee are to examine the application of the Declaration with a view to making suggestions and recommendations on the progress and extent of its implementation. The Committee, unlike the General Assembly, may hear individual petitioners and hold hearings in the field and in this way has functioned as an effective instrument of communication between the United Nations and unofficial groups. In particular, it has provided an invaluable forum for the views of the African nationalist leaders in Rhodesia.[23]

NOTES

1. See Hans Kelsen, "On Interpretation," Preface to The Law of the United Nations, Praeger, New York, 1950.

2. Ibid., pp. xiv-xv.

3. On formal and informal amendments of the Charter, see Ralph Zacklin, "Challenge of Rhodesia," International Conciliation No. 575, November 1969, pp. 116 ff. The first and only formal amendments to the Charter, to provide for the enlargement of the Economic and Social Council and the Security Council, were adopted in 1963. A general revision of the Charter is not considered to be politically feasible. Many states, particularly the permanent members of the Security Council, are reluctant to engage in an open-ended revision of the Charter system.

4. Ibid., pp. 171 ff.

5. For political reasons, the Security Council has sometimes refrained from making a strict determination under the terms of Article 39 as, for example, in the case of the Indonesian question (see United Nations Doc. S/459). For examples of strict determinations under Article 39, see the Palestine question (United Nations Doc. S/801 and S/902); the Korean question (United Nations Doc. S/1501); and the Congo (United Nations Doc. S/4741).

6. As in the case of Palestine, United Nations Doc. S/459 and S/801, op. cit.

7. Palestine, United Nations Doc. S/801.

8. The Congo, United Nations Doc. S/4387.

9. See United Nations Doc. S/1511.

10. See United Nations Doc. S/5575.

11. Security Council Resolution 181. See United Nations Doc. S/5386.

12. Security Council Resolution 182. See United Nations Doc. S/5471.

13. Security Council Resolutions 216 and 217.

14. United Nations General Assembly Resolution 377A (V), paragraph 1.

15. United Nations General Assembly Resolution 1761 (XVII).

16. United Nations General Assembly Resolution 2107 (XX).

17. United Nations General Assembly Resolution 288A (IV).

18. United Nations General Assembly Resolution 500 (V).

19. United Nations General Assembly Resolution 1807 (XVII).

20. United Nations General Assembly Resolution 1899 (XVIII).

21. See Zacklin, op. cit., pp. 188-195.

22. United Nations General Assembly Resolution 1654 (XVI), November 27, 1961.

23. The General Assembly has established a number of subsidiary organs which monitor the situation in Southern Africa on a permanent basis. The Special Committee on Decolonization (also referred to as the Committee of 24) is the most important of these subsidiary organs. Others are the Special Committee on Apartheid established by General Assembly Resolution 1761 (XVII) on November 6, 1962 "to keep the racial policies of the Government of South Africa under review" and the Council for Namibia established by General Assembly Resolution 2248 (S-V) of May 19, 1967 "to administer South West Africa until independence." The joint meeting of the three bodies was requested in General Assembly Resolution 2671 F (XXV) of December 8, 1970. In recent years, however, an estrangement between the African states and Western powers in the Decolonization Committee has developed, culminating in the withdrawal of both the United Kingdom and the United States from the Committee. The Committee in a sense is its own victim. Confronted by a frustrating disparity between formal pronouncements and implementation, it has resorted to a "programme of action," which has provoked the disintegration of the consultation procedures in the General Assembly.

7

THE UNFOLDING STRATEGY
OF SANCTIONS

Politically, the United Nations approach to the ultimate deployment of mandatory sanctions against Rhodesia has been determined
by the necessity of obtaining the required minimum political consensus
for the application of Chapter VII provisions, in other words, the
agreement or acquiescence of the five permanent members of the
Security Council. For this reason, the unfolding of sanctions has been
characterized by a painstaking and deliberate escalation from selective
optional sanctions through an intermediate stage of selective mandatory
sanctions reaching "comprehensive" mandatory sanctions, two and a
half years after the unilateral declaration of independence (UDI).

Legally and constitutionally, as we have seen, the adoption of
sanctions is contingent upon the formulation of a number of principles,
findings, and determinations by organs of the United Nations which
provide the legitimate basis for UN action. In the Rhodesian context,
these were, firstly, the elevation of self-determination to an internationally recognized and enforceable principle of a public policy
character, secondly, a determination that the Rhodesian question was
not exclusively within the domestic jurisdiction of the administering
state, and, thirdly, the finding that the Rhodesian situation represented
a threat to the peace.

During the decade of the fifties and in the sixties, the General
Assembly was instrumental in achieving the progressive development
of the principle of self-determination. From a rather modest beginning
in 1952, when the Assembly requested the Human Rights Commission
to give priority to the question of the right of peoples to self-determination [General Assembly Resolution 549 (VI)], the Assembly had
succeeded by 1960 in securing the adoption, without dissent, of the
Declaration on the Granting of Independence to Colonial Countries
and Peoples with its vigorous affirmation of the right of all peoples
to self-determination.[1] The right to self-determination has subsequently been reaffirmed by the General Assembly on several occasions,

notably in the Declaration on Principles of International Law concerning Friendly Relations and Cooperation Among States adopted by acclamation in 1970, which proclaims that by virtue of the principle of equal rights and self-determination of peoples, all peoples have the right freely to determine their political status and that states have a corresponding duty to promote the realization of the principle.[2]

Secondly, as we have seen in Part I, the Assembly characterized the Rhodesian situation as a matter of international concern when it affirmed in Resolution 1747 (XVI) of June 28, 1962 the nonselfgoverning status of the territory.[3]

As the threat to the peace inherent in a UDI loomed ever larger, consideration of the Rhodesian situation by the two principal organs of the United Nations—the General Assembly and the Security Council—gradually converged. Until 1965 the Security Council had not succeeded in developing the necessary consensus among the permanent members to enable it to undertake an initiative. Its only attempt to do so, in the autumn of 1963, failed when the United Kingdom vetoed a relatively innocuous proposal calling upon it not to transfer sovereignty or military forces to the Rhodesian regime.* In May 1965, however, the Security Council could no longer ignore the increasingly strident atmosphere created by Ian Smith and, in a resolution on which four of the five permanent members of the Security Council abstained, it requested the United Kingdom to take all necessary action to prevent a UDI.[4] In October 1965 the Security Council's request was reiterated by the General Assembly. After condemning in advance any attempt on the part of the Rhodesian authorities to seize independence by illegal means, and declaring that minority rule would be incompatible with the principle of equal rights and self-determination, the Assembly called upon the United Kingdom to take all possible measures to prevent a UDI and, in the event of such a declaration, to take all steps necessary to put an immediate end to the rebellion.[5]

The principal focus of the organization's pressure at this point was still the United Kingdom government, which continued to cling to the view that Rhodesia was a self-governing colony, rather than a nonselfgoverning territory within the terms of Chapter XI of the Charter, and that, therefore, the organization was not competent to discuss the matter. The seriousness with which the situation was now being regarded was reflected in the use of the formula "all necessary action," which implied at least ultimately the use of force. This was made explicit by a General Assembly Resolution adopted on November 5, 1965, which requested the United Kingdom, as the administering

---

*The United States and France abstained, and all eight other Security Council members voted in favor of the Resolution.

power, to carry out a number of measures including the release of political prisoners, the repeal of repressive and discriminatory legislation such as the Law and Order (maintenance) Act and the Land Apportionment Act, and the suspension of the 1961 Constitution. The United Kingdom was called upon to employ all necessary measures, including military force, to implement this request.[6]

This General Assembly Resolution was, however, nonbinding, and in any event the United Kingdom government had repeatedly emphasized that it was opposed to the use of force in Rhodesia, an attitude which was shared by several delegations fearful of the precedential effect of inviting a member state to use military force extraneous of Chapter VII of the Charter. Furthermore, British opposition to the use of force is bipartisan. Prime Minister Wilson underlined the essential compatibility of both major parties on this issue when addressing the Commonwealth Prime Ministers Conference in June 1965, although some Conservatives thought that they detected some equivocation in Mr. Wilson's position when in reply to a question in the House of Commons he had said: "The legal government of Rhodesia is the Governor. If the Governor were to approach Her Majesty's government for forces, police, or any other assistance to help restore law and order, we would, of course, respond to the request; we would naturally give very full consideration to it." As far as is known, however, there has never been any serious intention to deploy British troops against a rebellious Rhodesia, and the United Kingdom government has consistently vetoed any Security Council resolution calling for the use of military force by the administering power in Rhodesia.

The UDI on November 11, 1965 had one immediate and farreaching consequence on the international plane. The United Kingdom government now reversed its stand on the lack of competence of the United Nations, and seizing the initiative in order to forestall or outflank the expected deluge of African protests, it requested a meeting of the Security Council to consider the Rhodesian situation.

This pragmatic reversal of British policy, as the Foreign Secretary explained, was based on recognition of the fact that "an attempt to establish in Africa an illegal regime based on minority rule is a matter of world concern." Henceforth, Britain was obliged to recognize both its own responsibility and the legitimacy of the concerns of the international community in the formulation of its Rhodesian policy.

The first action of the Security Council in the wake of UDI was a call to all states not to accord recognition to the Smith regime and to refrain from rendering any assistance to it.[7] Although formal recognition is of doubtful significance today, it does constitute for a state in Rhodesia's situation an important element of symbolic acceptability as Ian Smith unwittingly revealed when in 1965 he erroneously asserted that recognition would be forthcoming from a number of states. In fact, Rhodesia has not been formally recognized by any member of the international community, including South Africa and Portugal.

Between November 12 and 20, 1965, the Security Council became enmeshed in the problem of finding a politically acceptable response to UDI. Predictably, the Council became a battleground between the forces of swift action and moderation. It finally turned back a draft resolution submitted by the Ivory Coast, which would have called for the implementation of enforcement measures provided for in Articles 41, 42, and 43 of the Charter, including military measures, and adopted instead a compromise resolution submitted by Bolivia and Uruguay. Resolution 217, which launched the first stage in the United Nations sanctions policy, received the affirmative votes of 10 members of the Council, only France abstaining, and despite the fact it fell considerably short of African demands, it nevertheless presented the Rhodesian situation in an entirely new light. In the first place, the Council made the crucial determination that Rhodesia constituted a threat to international peace and security, thereby paving the way for the implementation of Chapter VII provisions. Secondly, it declared the UDI to be of no legal validity. Thirdly, it called upon the United Kingdom government to quell the rebellion, thereby recognizing the United Kingdom's continuing responsibility for events in Rhodesia, and fourthly, it called upon all states to desist from providing Rhodesia with arms, equipment, military materials, and "to do their utmost in order to break all economic relations with Southern Rhodesia, including an embargo on oil and petroleum products." The effect of this resolution was to institute, for the first time in United Nations practice, sanctions, albeit optional, creating a partial interruption of economic relations under the terms of Article 41 of the Charter.[8]

The inadequacies and ineffectiveness of optional sanctions as a coercive instrument, expressively denounced by the African states prior to the adoption of this policy, soon emerged. In pursuance of Resolution 217, British air and naval forces had intensified their surveillance of vessels in the Mozambique Channel to prevent oil supplies from reaching Rhodesia via the Mozambique port of Beira. On April 4, 1966 the British frigate Plymouth intercepted, on the high seas, the Joanna V, a 12,920-ton oil tanker bound for Beira. The vessel, which was flying the Greek flag, was owned by a Panamanian corporation and chartered to a South African company. The text of Resolution 217 was transmitted by radio to the Captain of the Joanna V from the British vessel with instructions to change course. The Captain refused, stating that his cargo was destined for Djibouti in French Somaliland and that he wished to put into Beira merely for the purposes of taking on fresh supplies. The Joanna V reached Beira at dawn on April 5 and dropped anchor two miles offshore. In the midst of this unusually dramatic and newsworthy scenario, the United Kingdom requested an emergency meeting of the Security Council to consider proposals for preventing any oil from reaching Rhodesia in contravention of the embargo imposed by the United Kingdom in conformity with Security Council Resolution 217. Whether as a result of the worldwide publicity attendant upon the Joanna V or, as is more likely, because the United Kingdom, for once, acted with aggressive determination, the ensuing Security Council Resolution achieved the unprecedented distinction of invoking the enforcement provisions of Chapter VII of the Charter, authorizing the United Kingdom to use force, if necessary, to implement the 217 decision. Resolution 221 of April 9, 1966 called upon the United Kingdom "to prevent by the use of force if necessary the arrival at Beira of vessels reasonably believed to be carrying oil destined for Rhodesia" and authorized the arrest and detention of the Joanna V upon its departure from Beira should it discharge its cargo of oil. Such was the political conjuncture at the time that this Resolution obtained the affirmative support of three permanent members of the Security Council—the United Kingdom, the United States, and China—while the two others—France and the Soviet Union—abstained.[9] Within 24 hours of the adoption of Resolution 221, the British frigate Berwick intercepted the oil tanker Manuela some 150 miles southeast of Beira. The Manuela, which had been under surveillance for some time during which it had changed both its course and its ownership more than once, carried 16,000 tons of petroleum ostensibly destined for Rotterdam via Durban. The Captain of the Manuela offered no resistance to the interception of the vessel.

Notwithstanding the Security Council's demonstration of forcible measures and the deployment by the British government of its air and naval forces, it was nevertheless disturbingly apparent to the majority of the members of the General Assembly that measures that fell short of mandatory sanctions were inherently impotent. In particular, the Special Committee on Decolonization, habitually trenchant in these matters, recommended that the Security Council urgently consider wider employment of the measures permissable under Chapter VII. At the request of 32 African states, the Security Council did meet to consider a draft African resolution, which would have imposed mandatory sanctions and would have authorized the United Kingdom to use force to remove the Smith regime.[10] After a prolonged and often heated debate, held between May 17 and 23, in which proponents and opponents of collective enforcement action rehearsed the all too familiar arguments, the draft resolution failed to receive the necessary majority. Eight abstentions outweighed the six affirmative votes and a single negative vote.[11]

The use of force and the imposition of mandatory sanctions henceforth completely dominated discussion of the Rhodesian issue at the United Nations. The Twenty-first Session of the General Assembly appealed to the Security Council to "decide to apply the enforcement measures envisaged under Chapter VII of the Charter," and called upon the United Kingdom to use all measures, including in particular the use of force, to put an end to the illegal Rhodesian regime.12 This latter provision, submitted to a separate roll-call vote, demonstrated a substantial division of opinion among the members of the General Assembly. Thirty-five states either voted against or abstained from voting on this issue. For the most part they feared that the effectiveness of economic sanctions would be undermined if forcible measures were to be recommended but not employed and, more importantly, in the unlikely event that such measures were employed, serious repercussions might ensue for the African population in Rhodesia and for the United Nations itself. Unpleasant memories of the Congo operation were no doubt still fresh in the minds of many delegates, and the Rhodesian armed forces, probably correctly, are generally regarded as a well-equipped, well-trained, and highly disciplined force.* In the course of the General Assembly debate, however, the United Kingdom representative categorically asserted that if the Rhodesian regime did not bring the rebellion to an end, Britain would sponsor a Security Council resolution calling for selective mandatory sanctions. The British government's injunction to the Rhodesian regime must have appeared rather naive to Ian Smith and his followers, particularly in view of the fact that force would not be used. Furthermore, emboldened by their success in countering optional sanctions, the threat of mandatory sanctions was unlikely to produce a credible deterrent.

Selective mandatory sanctions were eventually imposed by Security Council Resolution 232 of December 16, 1966. By 11 affirmative votes with 4 abstentions, the Council found that the situation in Rhodesia constituted "a threat to international peace and security" and decided that all member states shall prevent trade with Rhodesia on certain specified commodities, including oil.13 Resolution 232 established a new precedent in United Nations practice, for it was the first time in the history of the organization that the Security Council had called for mandatory sanctions under Articles 39 and 41 of the Charter. Failure or refusal to implement this Resolution, which was a Council decision, would entail a violation of Article 25 of the Charter, under which members agreed to accept and carry out decisions of the Council.

---

*In 1964 the Rhodesian armed forces included 60 fighter bombers and attack aircraft and an army of 3,400 men. These effectives have since been reinforced with assistance from South Africa.

The second phase of the United Nations sanctions policy, which came into effect on December 16, 1966, was designed principally to prevent the export from Rhodesia of its most important products and commodities: asbestos, iron ore, chrome, pig iron, sugar, tobacco, copper, meat, skins, and leather. Resolution 232 also placed an embargo on exports to Rhodesia of arms, ammunition, military vehicles of all kinds, aircraft, motor vehicles, and oil or oil products.

Notwithstanding the imposition of selective mandatory sanctions, there was no immediate sign of any appreciable weakening of the Smith regime. An obviously frustrated Special Committee on Decolonization met in Zambia in June 1967 and expressed the view that to be credible, sanctions must be comprehensive, mandatory, and backed by force on the part of the administering power. The Committee condemned the governments of South Africa and Portugal for their blatant defiance of General Assembly and Security Council Resolutions and recommended to the Security Council that it take the necessary measures under Chapter VII of the Charter to strengthen the sanctions policy.[14]

It was not until several months later, however, in March 1968, that the Security Council resumed consideration of the Rhodesian situation. The event that brought about another important shift in policy was the execution of three African common law prisoners. The executions were unlawful under British law because the Queen had granted a commutation of sentence. The Smith regime nevertheless chose to demonstrate its independence from the Crown through this action. A month later the United Kingdom presented a draft resolution to the Security Council calling for comprehensive sanctions.

On May 29, 1968, the Council unanimously decided to impose comprehensive mandatory sanctions and to establish a committee to examine reports on the implementation of the Resolution. Given its scope and nature, it is significant that Resolution 253 was unanimously adopted—an event which is rare enough under normal circumstances but doubly impressive in the instant case.

Operative paragraphs 3, 4, and 5, "in furtherance of the objective of ending the rebellion," impose on member states a series of obligations to prevent the import into their territories of all commodities and products originating in Rhodesia, the sale or supply of commodities and products to Rhodesia, the carriage of goods in vessels or aircraft of their registration to or from Rhodesia, investment, public or private, in Rhodesia, entry into their territories of any person traveling on a Rhodesian passport, and airline operations to or linking with Rhodesia. The new sanctions admitted of very few exceptions (on medical and humanitarian grounds).[15]

Resolution 253 represented a watershed political consensus on Rhodesia that has not been approached since. In retrospect, it would appear to have been the effective ceiling of collective measures, although the African states have persistently attempted to expand the scope and effectiveness of sanctions. For the African bloc, in particular, Resolution 253 was too little, too late. In 1968 only a few months after the implementation of comprehensive sanctions, the General Assembly concluded a review of the situation by stating that sanctions would not bring an end to the rebellion unless they were strictly supervised and complied with, in particular, by South Africa and Portugal. Once again, it called upon the government of the United Kingdom to use force to put an end to the illegal regime in Rhodesia, noting the offers of Zambia and the Congo (now Zaire) to make available their territories and airspace for this purpose.[16]

In June 1969, a joint draft resolution submitted to the Security Council by Algeria, Nepal, Pakistan, Senegal, and Zambia, which would have extended the 253 sanctions to the territories of South Africa and Mozambique, failed to receive the necessary majority by only one vote. The narrow margin of defeat raised false hopes over the possibility of expanding the scope of sanctions to include Mozambique and even South Africa, but these have proved illusory. Since 1969 the Security Council has, in fact, been unable to do more than reaffirm its previous Resolutions and exhort member states to observe the mandatory sanctions already agreed upon.[17] Worse still, the Council has witnessed a serious erosion of support for its policy of comprehensive mandatory sanctions dramatized by the open violation of the terms of Resolution 253 by the United States—a permanent member of the Council.

In the meantime, the Rhodesian regime has consolidated its internal position. In a constitutional referendum carried out among the white minority on June 20, 1969, proposals for a new Constitution were carried, nearly every clause of which disclosed racial discrimination, oppression, and injustice. About 55,000 people, or approximately 1 percent of the total population, approved of the new Republican Constitution, which provides for strict racial separation and permanent white supremacy.

The year 1973 then is a far cry from the optimism of 1968 when Prime Minister Wilson declared that the capitulation of the Smith regime was a matter of weeks, not months.

The elapsed period of five years has demonstrated both the unexpected resilience of the Smith regime, thanks largely to the cooperation of its South African neighbors, and the strengths and weaknesses of collective measures. Through it all, however, one fact emerges, namely, the growing resistance of the African majority to a system of government that deprives them of the most elementary human rights.

In light of the de facto renunciation of its responsibility toward the 5.3 million Africans by Britain, the United Nations' primary

responsibility to maintain international peace and security requires
it to persevere in the enforcement of sanctions against Rhodesia until
such time as the objectives of the sanctions policy have been attained.

NOTES

1. See United Nations General Assembly Resolution 1514 (XV),
operative paragraph 2: "All peoples have the right to self-determination; by virtue of that right they freely determine their political status
and freely pursue their economic, social and cultural development."
United Nations General Assembly Resolutions, Fifteenth Session, Vol.
I, p. 67. The General Assembly vote on Resolution 1514 (XV) was 89
in favor, none against, and 9 abstentions.

2. United Nations General Assembly Resolution 2625 (XXV).
See also United Nations General Assembly Resolutions 545 (VI), 637A
(VII), 837 (IX), 1188 (XII), 2131 (XX), 2144A (XXI), 2160 (XX), and
2588B (XXIV).

3. The operative parts of this resolution requested the administering authority (the United Kingdom) to convene a constitutional
conference, with participation of the representatives of all political
parties, for the purpose of formulating a constitution in place of the
1961 Constitution, which would ensure the rights of the majority of
the people, on the basis of "one man, one vote." See United Nations
General Assembly Resolutions, Sixteenth Session, Vol. II, 1962, p. 3.

4. Security Council Resolution 202.

5. United Nations General Resolution 2012 (XX).

6. United Nations General Assembly Resolution 2022 (XX).

7. Security Council Resolution 216 (1965), November 12, 1965,
adopted by a vote of 10 in favor, none against, and 1 abstention
(France).

8. For the full text of Security Council Resolution 217 (1965) of
November 20, 1965, see Security Council Official Records: 20th Year,
pp. 8-9.

9. Security Council Resolution 221, April 9, 1966. Those voting
in favor were Argentina, China, Japan, Jordan, Netherlands, New
Zealand, Nigeria, Uganda, the United Kingdom, and the United States.
Those abstaining were Bulgaria, France, Mali, USSR, and Uruguay.

10. See United Nations Doc. S/7285 and Add. 2 of May 10, 1966.

11. See United Nations Doc. S/7285 and Add. 1, draft resolution
submitted by Mali, Nigeria, and Uganda. Those in favor were Bulgaria,
Jordan, Mali, Nigeria, Uganda, and USSR. The eight abstentions were
Argentina, China, France, Japan, Netherlands, United Kingdom, United
States, and Uruguay. The only negative vote was cast by New Zealand.

12. United Nations General Assembly Resolution 2151 (XXI), adopted by 89 votes to 2 with 17 abstentions.

13. Security Council Resolution 232, December 16, 1966. See United Nations Doc. S/7621 and Rev. 1 (UK draft) and S/7630 and Corr. 1 and Rev. 1 (Mali, Nigeria, and Uganda amendment). The four abstentions were Bulgaria, France, Mali, and USSR.

14. These views were subsequently embodied in General Assembly Resolution 2262 (XXII) of November 3, 1967.

15. For the full text of this Resolution, see Security Council Official Records: 23rd Year, pp. 5-7.

16. United Nations General Assembly Resolution 2383 (XXIII), November 7, 1968.

17. See, for example, Security Council Resolutions 277, 288, 314, 318, and 320.

The intervention of the Security Council in the Rhodesian case and its implementation of the provisions of Chapter VII of the Charter are unique events in the annals of the United Nations and will almost certainly have profound consequences for the future development of the organization. As we pass from the examination of the institutional and legal aspects of the Rhodesian situation to the issues raised by the practical implementation of sanctions, it may be useful to pause briefly to consider the political framework within which the United Nations policies have been formulated.

The politics of sanctions cannot be divorced from the larger issue of which Rhodesia is inextricably a part, namely, the decolonization of Africa and the struggle against apartheid. Both north and south of the Zambezi River, Rhodesia is perceived as a central bastion in the line reaching from Angola to Mozambique. Within this southern part of the African Continent are concentrated the last remaining vestiges of nineteenth-century colonialism. In Angola and Mozambique, the Portuguese continue to practice their distinctive brand of racial harmony,[1] while in South West Africa (Namibia) and South Africa, apartheid is rigidly enforced in a police-state which permits no deviation. Decolonization and the situation in South Africa have, therefore, been the preeminent concern of the African states in the United Nations.[2] As we have seen, the African states achieved satisfaction on the decolonization issue to a remarkable degree, and by 1965, when the Rhodesian situation first appeared on the Security Council agenda, they combined an overwhelming majority in the General Assembly with an astute usage of the organizations's machinery. Rhodesia was, therefore, a challenge for the African states and a test of the limits of their new-found political strength. The African purchase over the General Assembly was successfully demonstrated in 1962 with the adoption of Resolution 1747 (XVI), but the translation of this plenary power into the executive power of the Security Council is an entirely different matter.

Since May 1965, the Security Council has adopted 13 resolutions on Rhodesia.[3] Throughout this period, the African states represented on the Council have established an impressive solidarity with the states of Asia and Latin America as well as with the nonpermanent Commonwealth and western European members. The five permanent members have divided along familiar lines. The United Kingdom, cast in the reluctant role of the administering power, has with the support of the United States exercised a moderating influence on the urgent demands of the African states, resisting, in particular, all demands for the use of force. Arrayed against the Atlantic allies, China and the Soviet Union have unequivocally supported the most extreme African position. Only France, of the five permanent members, adopted a neutral position for some years before bringing to an end its position of principle, which was, in fact, a hangover from the Algerian War.

The political alignment in the Security Council and its dialectical style have changed very little over the years. Resolution 202 of May 6, 1965, which was the first Security Council Resolution on Rhodesia and which requested the United Kingdom government to take all necessary action to prevent a UDI, was adopted with a bare majority of seven to nothing with four abstentions by permanent members of the Council. Those voting in favor were Bolivia, China, Ivory Coast, Jordan, Malaysia, the Netherlands, and Uruguay. The manner in which the four abstentions were explained is instructive. The United Kingdom representative, Lord Caradon, rested his argument on the lack of competence of the United Nations in matters of domestic jurisdiction.[4] Ambassador Seydoux of France also embraced this argument, but in order to mollify the Francophone states, he added that "we disagree on the competence of the Organization, but not on the need to have done with delaying tactics (sic), dissimulations, and half measures. . . ."[5] Ambassador Stevenson of the United States, after asserting that the Resolution "was constructive in both spirit and intent," nevertheless found certain "difficulties" with it. The Resolution was in his view "somewhat unbalanced in that it focuses entirely on the United Kingdom."[6] Having regard to the fact that the United Kingdom itself at that time insisted that the situation in Rhodesia was a matter of domestic jurisdiction (although one which inconveniently it was unable to do anything about), it is a little difficult to see which other states the Security Council's Resolution could have addressed. Finally, Mr. Federenko of the Soviet Union explained his country's abstention on the ground that the Resolution was "obviously inadequate." The principal amendment to the Resolution, which had been introduced by the Soviet Union, had called for the immediate granting of independence to Rhodesia, an entirely impractical and, in the circumstances, foolhardy option, which the Soviet Union knew the United Kingdom would never be irresponsible enough to adopt but which it proposed expressly for the purpose of obliging the United Kingdom to reject. In this manner, Mr. Federenko would be able to denounce Lord Caradon for "(raising) his hand against the immediate abolition of the colonial regime. . . ."[7]

Some months later, as we have seen above, the United Kingdom abandoned its objections based on the domestic jurisdiction argument, a move which did not prevent France from clinging to its position for three more years. The Soviet Union, on the other hand, appears to have found its original strategy eminently satisfactory and for more than eight years has mined a rich vein, supporting African demands while at the same time excoriating Britain, the United States, and other imperialists. The United Kingdom and the United States have participated throughout in a curiously symbiotic relationship which, as far as the United States is concerned, would seem to defy even political expediency. The two have voted together on every Rhodesian Resolution save one since 1965. The single exception is Resolution 318 of July 28, 1972, which condemned all acts in violation of the sanctions Resolutions. The Resolution was adopted by 14 votes in favor and the United States abstained. In September 1972, however, the United Kingdom joined the United States in abstaining on a Resolution which specifically urged the United States to cooperate fully with the United Nations and more recently, as we shall see in some detail below, the two countries jointly vetoed a 1973 Resolution which would have strengthened sanctions.

With regard to the three sanctions Resolutions—217, 232, and 253—France abstained on the first, four states abstained on the second (France, Mali, Bulgaria, and the USSR), and only Resolution 253, which established comprehensive mandatory sanctions, was unanimously approved.

Gradually, the United Kingdom and the United States have become increasingly isolated from the mainstream in the Security Council. The French government abandoned its technical reservations on United Nations competence in 1968 when it voted in favor of Resolution 253. The admission of the People's Republic of China has brought greatly increased support to the African cause, and the Soviet Union is making every effort to ensure that it is not politically outflanked by the Chinese. In these circumstances, the United Kingdom and the United States have resorted increasingly to the veto.

The politics of sanctions are, therefore, a lesson in the limits of influence. Possessing an overwhelming majority in the General Assembly and an automatic majority in the Security Council, the African states have been frustrated in their attempts to activate the full force of United Nations collective measures. They have learned, as David Kay has remarked that

> At its present stage of development the United Nations generally can have a significant international impact only to the extent that there is a congruence of influence patterns in the Organization and in the external international political environment. To the extent that this congruence is absent, a group may have influence within the Organization sufficient to shape the policy outputs of the Organization but still be unable to obtain the fulfillment of the demands made in such outputs. This is largely the situation in which the new nations currently find themselves.[8]

NOTES

1. The Times of London carried detailed allegations of atrocities carried out by Portuguese forces in Mozambique in 1971-72 in its edition of July 10, 1973. See also Bulletin No. 19 of United Nations and Southern Africa, United Nations Office of Public Information, New York, July 1973.

2. For a detailed analysis of issues of concern to African states in the United Nations, see David Kay, The New Nations in the United Nations, 1960-1967, Columbia University Press, New York, 1970, pp. 45-50.

3. See Appendix A.

4. Security Council Official Records: 20th Year, 1965, 1202nd meeting, Vol. I, pp. 17-18.

5. Ibid., p. 19.

6. Ibid., p. 20.

7. Ibid., p. 21.

8. Kay, op. cit., p. 187.

THE THEORY AND REALITY
OF INTERNATIONAL SANCTIONS

THE CONDITIONS
AND CONSEQUENCES OF
INTERNATIONAL IMPLEMENTATION

Security Council decisions taken under Chapter VII of the Charter, although legally binding on all members of the United Nations in accordance with Article 25, are not directly applicable or self-executing within the jurisdiction of member states.[1] At the present stage of development of the international legal order, the implementation of international decisions requires the intervention of the appropriate domestic agency. Consequently, the inescapable vice of international enforcement is that it is of necessity highly decentralized, assuming the form of unilateral, but hopefully contemporaneous, implementation of international decisions through domestic organs of states. In other words, the legal obligation to perform or to refrain from performing certain acts incumbent upon states by virtue of Security Council decisions is contingent for its execution upon the executive, administrative, legislative, or judicial action of each individual state in accordance with each state's political and constitutional system.

The accumulated evidence that may be derived from the experience of the League of Nations and the United Nations suggests that collective economic and other nonforceful measures are unlikely to be successful unless certain minimum conditions are fulfilled. The economic measures applied by the League of Nations against Italy during the Italo-Ethiopian War of 1935 were notoriously unsuccessful, and even in circumstances of total warfare during World War II, the Allied measures against Germany, as Albert Speer has related, did not succeed in cutting off strategic supplies.[2] A 1965 analysis of Apartheid and United Nations Collective Measures,[3] prepared under the auspices of the Carnegie Endowment, outlined the minimum requirements for an effective economic embargo as follows:

. . . prompt application, all inclusive support, effective administration and enforcement, mutual aid to the damaged partners, and retention of the measures as long as [is] necessary to secure compliance by the offending state.[4]

To this might be added, although it is undoubtedly implicit, the requirements of comprehensiveness and international monitoring or control. As we have already seen (Part II), the manner in which sanctions were progressively imposed upon Rhodesia between 1965 and 1968 violated the first requisite—of prompt application. In this part of the study, the diverse problems of enforcement encountered in collective action initiated in an imperfectly organized legal order will be examined.

UNIVERSALITY

It is axiomatic that international sanctions cannot succeed unless rigorously and universally enforced. The universal enforcement of Rhodesian sanctions has been problematical, and largely hypothetical, from their inception. In the first place, the United Nations itself has been conspicuously lacking in universality, and secondly, for the reasons already cited, noncompliance cannot be sanctioned with any greater effect than that applied against the original sanctionee.

Although the admission of China to the United Nations in 1971 finally terminated the most obvious infraction of the principle of United Nations' universality, the organization is still universal in name only. With regard to the enforcement of sanctions, the two most important nonmember states are the Federal Republic of Germany and Switzerland.[5] The Federal Republic was Rhodesia's largest European trading partner prior to unilateral declaration of independence (UDI),* while Switzerland, although a relatively minor trading partner, is strategically well situated to serve as an entrepôt for transshipment of Rhodesian exports. The question of third-party obligations under treaties in this situation transcends, therefore, the theoretical and doctrinal considerations and raises issues of the most practical kind.

As a general rule, a treaty cannot impose obligations or rights upon a third party without its consent. The recently concluded Vienna Convention on the Law of Treaties, which codified the rules and practices of treaty law, expressed the general rule on third-party

----

*The Federal Republic's imports from Rhodesia in 1965 were worth slightly more than $35 million. Exports totaled $10.9 million.

obligations as follows (Article 34): "A treaty does not create either obligations or rights for a third state without its consent." The Vienna Convention does, however, permit a number of exceptions to the general rule. In the first place, an obligation may arise for a third state from a provision of a treaty if it is the intention of the parties to the treaty that this be so and if the third state expressly accepts that obligation in writing.[6] Secondly, the Vienna Convention recognizes that a treaty rule may always become binding on a third state if the rule should become recognized as a customary rule of international law.[7] Since many of the fundamental principles of the Charter of the United Nations are recognized as having a customary international law character, it follows that they are binding on all states whether members of the United Nations or not. This would not seem, however, to provide a sufficient legal basis for imposing obligations arising under Chapter VII of the Charter upon nonmembers of the United Nations, particularly since, as in the case of Switzerland, the incompatibility of Chapter VII obligations with its political neutrality is the principal reason for nonmembership.

In its efforts to secure the widest possible implementation of sanctions, the Security Council has restored to diverse strategems and justifications in order to buttress its position. In particular, the Security Council has sought to extend its sanctions policy to the broadest number of states by virtue of the formula "members of the United Nations or of the Specialized Agencies." This category embraces virtually all members of the international community at the present time. It should be noted, however, that in so doing the Security Council has distinguished very carefully between decisions that are directed exclusively to members of the United Nations and requests that are directed to members of the United Nations or of the Specialized Agencies. Thus, for example, in Security Council Resolution 253 (1968) of May 29, 1968, the operative paragraphs that have the character of decisions—paragraphs 3 to 7—are addressed exclusively to members of the United Nations. Paragraphs 8, 9, 14, 15, 18, and 22, which employ the more comprehensive formula, are framed as requests. In addressing such requests to third states, the United Nations is acting in accordance with Article 2, paragraph 6, of the Charter, which provides that

> the organization shall ensure that states which are not members of the United Nations act in accordance with these principles so far as may be necessary for the maintenance of international peace and security.

Since the Security Council has declared the situation in Rhodesia to be a threat to the peace and since the measures decided upon by the Security Council are obviously intended to maintain international peace and security, the observance of sanctions by third states would come under the principle embodied in Article 2, paragraph 5, on referral from paragraph 6. Finally, third-party obligations, it can be argued, arise from the fact that in imposing sanctions upon Rhodesia, the United Nations is enforcing a rule of international public policy from which there can be no derogation.

Thus, although there do seem to be some legal grounds for third-party enforcement of sanctions against Rhodesia, an examination of United Nations practice, particularly Security Council Resolutions, does seem to indicate that the United Nations rests its case more on the moral than the legal obligations of third states.

COMPREHENSIVENESS

The policy of sanctions as it has unfolded has been designed primarily to attain two short-term objectives: the economic strangulation of Rhodesia and, concurrently with this, the total political and diplomatic isolation of the regime.

As far as economic measures are concerned, the objective of Security Council Resolution 253 as we have seen was to provoke as far as possible a complete cessation of trade with the outside world. The practical effect of these measures, in theory, has been to deny Rhodesia markets for its principal exports of asbestos, iron ore, chrome, pig iron, sugar, tobacco, copper, meat and meat products, hides, and skins and leather, as well as the export to Rhodesia of such essential items as oil and oil products, arms and military equipment, aircraft, motor vehicles, tractors, and manufacturing equipment. This is a formidable schedule of items, and the optimists who believed that the Rhodesian economy could not possibly withstand such deprivation may possibly be excused for believing that capitulation was only just around the corner.

The political and diplomatic isolation of the regime has been equally severe. As noted earlier, nonrecognition has been successfully maintained since 1965.[8] Nevertheless, Rhodesia maintains a number of representational missions abroad including two "diplomatic missions" in Pretoria and Lisbon, two "consulates" in Capetown and Beira, one "consulate" in Lourenco Marques, two "trade missions" in Johannesburg and Luanda, and an "information office" in Washington, D.C.[9] The geographic distribution of these missions, as we shall see below, reflects circumstantially the pattern of evasion of sanctions employed by Rhodesia since 1965.

Additional measures of isolation made mandatory by Security Council Resolution 253 include the nonrecognition of Rhodesian passports and the nonadmission of Rhodesian passport holders or persons suspected of residing in Rhodesia into the territories of member states and a ban on national airlines or aircraft, either registered or chartered in member states, from operating to or from Rhodesia.

The only exceptions allowed under Resolution 253 relate to supplies intended strictly for medical purposes, educational equipment, and material for use in schools and other educational institutions, publications, news material, and, in special humanitarian circumstances, foodstuffs. Similar exceptions exist for payments of pensions and for humanitarian, medical, or educational purposes. Short of abolishing these exceptions, which surely cannot be countenanced, it does not seem possible to go beyond the sanctions established by Resolution 253, though calls for so doing are periodically made.[10]

THE HOSTAGE STATE

It is probably inevitable that international sanctions on the Rhodesian scale cannot be implemented without causing economic hardship to some states and considerable inconvenience to others. Rhodesia's geography virtually guarantees a major disruption of the traditional patterns of trade in central Africa, particularly for contiguous states such as Zambia and Botswana, or trade-linked states such as Zaire and Malawi, all of which are struggling to attain even minimum developmental goals. The most severely affected of these is Zambia. Partly because of its geographical situation and partly due to trade patterns developed during the colonial period, the Zambian economy prior to UDI was overwhelmingly dependent on Rhodesian and South African commercial interests. Zambia's complete dependence on the Rhodesian transportation system via ports in Mozambique and South Africa as well as Rhodesian sources of coal, coke, and electrical energy predicated economic dislocation on a grand scale including among other things the rerouting of import-export traffic away from ports in Mozambique and the rail route through Rhodesia. To comply with its obligations under the sanctions Resolutions, Zambia is required to do the following: reroute copper exports, its principal foreign exchange earner, through more expensive and less reliable routes; seek new and more costly sources of coal required for the operation of its copper mines; replace the Beira-Umtali oil pipeline with alternative supply routes via Dar-es Salaam; and construct a new electrical generating plant on the Kariba Dam.

It is fair to say that since UDI, Zambia has been in a virtual state of siege as a consequence of the Rhodesian sanctions. Compliance with the sanctions policy by Zambia has depleted its foreign exchange reserves, increased the cost of living in Zambia, and retarded

Zambia's overall development plans. Very few governments and fewer leaders have the national support and personal conviction to subject their country to such a test in the name of international law.

To the extent that the San Francisco Conference considered the problem, it provided very inadequately for the remedy. Articles 49 and 50 of the Charter provide the legal basis for a collective remedy. The general principle is established in Article 49, which states: "The members of the United Nations shall join in affording mutual assistance in carrying out the measures decided upon by the Security Council." Article 50 establishes the procedure whereby the general principle may be implemented:

> If preventive or enforcement measures against any state
> are taken by the Security Council, any other state, whether
> a member of the United Nations or not, which finds itself
> confronted with special economic problems arising from
> the carrying out of those measures shall have the right
> to consult the Security Council with regard to a solution
> of those problems.

Since a state in this position would have the right to bring its problems to the attention of the Security Council in any event, Article 50 is somewhat redundant.

Resolution 253 expressly recognized Zambia's special problems by requesting member states of the United Nations and the Specialized Agencies, organizations within the United Nations system, and other international organizations "to extend assistance to Zambia as a matter of priority with a view to helping her solve such special economic problems as she may be confronted with arising from the carrying out of these decisions." The Security Council call for voluntary assistance has gone largely unheeded, however. Modest assistance to Zambia has been provided by the British government, the Scandanavian countries, and the United Nations Development Program, but generally speaking, the response of the international community to Zambia's plight has been apathetic. In a report to the Secretary-General on October 4, 1968, the Zambian government stated: "The Government of the Republic of Zambia reports with regret that no United Nations member states or organizations have offered Zambia assistance as the result of this [253] Resolution. The Zambian Government has had to bear all the costs with only a little help from the British Government at the start of the emergency."[11]

The Zambian policy of pursuing the implementation of sanctions to the maximum extent contrasts sharply with Botswana and Malawi, both of which informed the Security Council in 1968 that in the absence of substantial assistance from the United Nations, they would be unable to comply with sanctions.

Recently published figures indicate that in 1969, about 64 percent of Zambia's imports and 56.5 percent of its total exports transited Rhodesian railways and road haulage. By 1972, as a result of rerouting, only 45 percent of Zambia's imports came in through Rhodesia, but 53 percent of its exports still exited via Rhodesian railways.[12]

If collective economic measures are applied by the United Nations in execution of lawfully adopted Security Council Resolutions, states must, if such a system is to retain its credibility, assume all the obligations and burdens that arise from the implementation of such actions both individually and collectively. The lessons of the failure of the League of Nations in this respect should not be forgotten.

After several years of almost complete indifference to the Zambian plight, the issue was dramatically revived in January 1973 with the closing of the Zambian border by the Rhodesian authorities. Ironically, this action, which was intended as a short-term warning to Zambia, has probably inadvertently resulted in increasing the effect of sanctions on the Rhodesian economy. Furthermore, the border closure served to reopen the debate on the effectiveness of sanctions, and in focusing the attention of the international community upon the situation in southern Africa, it has resulted in a new phase in the sanctions policy.

In a letter to the President of the Security Council dated January 24, 1973, the Permanent Representative of Zambia to the United Nations requested an urgent meeting of the Council to consider "serious acts of aggression . . . committed by the white minority, illegal and racist regime in the British Colony of Southern Rhodesia." The Zambian Representative alleged that Rhodesian forces had committed numerous acts of subversion and sabotage against Zambia, that Rhodesian forces had been supplemented by 4,000 men from South Africa, and that on January 9, 1973 Rhodesia had closed the border between Zambia and Rhodesia.[13]

The Security Council considered Zambia's complaint between January 29 and February 2, 1973. In presenting his government's complaint, the Representative of Zambia declared that the closure of the border was an act of aggression by a regime whose racist policies had been condemned by the international community and against which the United Nations had imposed mandatory sanctions.[14] He alleged that the military incursions into Zambia from Rhodesia and the multiplication of incidents involving border crossings, shooting, and the planting of land mines in Zambian territory represented a major escalation of the conflict in southern Africa. Referring specifically to the mandatory sanctions against Rhodesia, the Zambian

Representative stated that his government had decided to establish permanent alternative routes for its imports and exports and to abandon the southern route altogether, thus eliminating a long-standing excuse resorted to by some states for not applying comprehensive mandatory sanctions.[15]

On February 1 the Representative of Sudan introduced two draft resolutions co-sponsored by Guinea, Kenya, and Yugoslavia, the first of which contained proposals concerning the political aspects of the complaint by Zambia,[16] while the second addressed itself to the problems of assistance to Zambia in the establishment of permanent alternative trade routes.[17]

By Resolution 326 (1973) adopted on February 2, 1973, the Security Council established a Special Mission, consisting of four members of the Security Council, to assess the political situation in the area and to report to the Council by March 1, 1973.* The Special Mission was also requested to assess the needs of Zambia in maintaining alternative systems of road, rail, air, and sea communications for the normal flow of traffic. For this latter purpose, it was assisted by a team of six United Nations experts.

The Special Mission held consultations with the authorities in the United Kingdom, Zambia, Tanzania, and Kenya and visited the border between Zambia and Rhodesia. Parallel to these political consultations, the economic experts consulted with their counterparts in Zambia, Kenya, and Tanzania and visited various ports and railroad installations under consideration for use in rerouting Zambian traffic from the south.

Assessing the political situation, the Special Mission concluded that the solution lay in the application of majority rule in Rhodesia, the strict implementation of mandatory sanctions against the illegal regime, and the implementation of relevant resolutions of the Security Council with regard to southern Africa as a whole. The measures announced by Zambia were deemed to be in accordance with the Security Council Resolutions, a finding of deceptive simplicity but actually of considerable importance in view of the attitude of certain states that the border closure was an "internal affair."[18]

The Special Mission issued a comprehensive report concerning Zambia's needs in maintaining alternative systems of communications on March 6, 1973.[19] The report addressed itself to the "normal flow of traffic," which was defined as "the amounts of imports and exports which would allow the citizens of Zambia to maintain their normal standard of living and allow the economy to develop in a

---

*Adopted by 13 votes in favor and 2 abstentions: the United Kingdom and the United States.

normal fashion, i.e., as if the special situation had not arisen."[20] On
this basis it was agreed that the normal flow of imports (excluding pipeline traffic) amounted to approximately 120,000 tons per month, while
the normal flow of exports amounted to between 68,000 tons and 80,000
tons per month.[21]

Of the total of 120,000 tons per month of imports, approximately
75,000 tons had previously been brought into Zambia via Rhodesia.
This tonnage must now be diverted to alternative land routes through
Zaire, Malawi, or Tanzania or be imported by air.* Capital requirements for the overland routes through Zambia, Malawi, and Tanzania
(for the provision of trucking units, rolling stock, handling equipment, storage facilities, workshops and maintenance facilities, and
radio communications equipment plus the cost of providing for personnel) were estimated by the experts at $124 million. Air freight
costs to bring in the balance of 15,000 tons per month were estimated
at $6.5 million per month. In addition to financing, it was noted that
significant amounts of technical assistance including operational
personnel would be needed and that the higher transport costs arising
from the use of alternative routes would total approximately $62
million annually. These increased costs would inflate the price levels
in Zambia, the cost structure in the mining sector, and the government deficit. In addition, the foreign exchange costs to Zambia of
transporting imports and exports would nearly double. The Special
Mission noted, however, that the equipment and facilities required
would be necessary in the normal course of development of Zambia,
Tanzania, and Malawi. To some extent, therefore, the capital investment merely reflects an earlier phasing of later developmental
needs.[22]

The report presented to the Security Council by the Special
Mission is noteworthy for a number of reasons. Firstly, it was
completed in little more than a month which, given the complexity
of the problems analyzed, the number of governments involved, and
the interdisciplinary nature of the information condensed, is a tribute
to the United Nations' capacity. Secondly, the report is unanimous.
Thirdly, it confirms that Zambia's complaint was justified and,
finally, that the Zambian problem and the situation of Africans in

---

*The Special Mission estimated that the Zaire route should
be capable of carrying 23,000 tons per month, the Malawi route
17,000 tons, and the Tanzanian route 65,000 tons if adequate assistance is provided. This would leave a short fall of some 15,000 tons
of imports each month to be brought in by air to maintain the normal
flow of traffic.

Rhodesia, in particular, and southern Africa, in general, are inextricably interwined.

On March 10, 1973, the Security Council approved two Resolutions based on the political and economic assessments of the Special Mission, respectively. A Resolution jointly sponsored by Guinea, India, Indonesia, Kenya, Panama, Peru, Sudan, and Yugoslavia concerning the political assessments was approved by a vote of 13 in favor with 2 abstentions—the United Kingdom and the United States.[23] This Resolution endorsed the conclusions of the Special Mission and, in particular, urged the United Kingdom government to convene, as soon as possible, a national constitutional conference where genuine representatives of the people of Zimbabwe (Rhodesia) as a whole would be able to work out a settlement relating to the future of the territory.

The Economic Resolution, sponsored by the same group of states, commended the government of Zambia for deciding to abandon the use of the southern route until majority rule is established in Rhodesia and, after taking note of the urgent economic needs of Zambia as indicated in the report of the Special Mission, appealed to all states for immediate technical, financial, and material assistance to Zambia, and requested the United Nations and its Specialized Agencies to assist Zambia in the areas identified in the report. Finally, the Resolution requested the Secretary-General, in collaboration with appropriate organizations of the United Nations system, to organize, with immediate effect, all forms of financial, technical, and material assistance to Zambia and requested the Economic and Social Council to consider periodically the question of economic assistance to Zambia as envisaged in this Resolution. The Economic Resolution was unanimously adopted.[24]

From the legal point of view, the Economic Resolution adopted on March 10, 1973 does not go any further than previous Resolutions 253 (1968) and 277 (1970), which also requested assistance for Zambia. It remains to be seen whether the strong moral obligation which this resolution creates will receive greater support from the international community in the light of the Special Mission's report. A number of African countries have already indicated their support for Zambia and have made either monetary contributions, as in the case of Zaire, or have made available facilities as in the case of Kenya and Tanzania.

As the Special Mission report indicates, to meet the short-term economic requirements of Zambia, very substantial financial and technical assistance is required, which clearly cannot be provided by, nor should it be expected of, developing states in Africa. The bulk of this assistance must, therefore, come from the industrialized countries including the Soviet Union, the United States, and the United

Kingdom. Unfortunately, the Security Council debate on the Economic
Resolution is less than encouraging in this respect. Doubts were
expressed concerning the authority of the Security Council to enter
the field of economic relations or of economic development, and it
was implied by some delegations that the Security Council has no
authority to direct requests to the Specialized Agencies to render
assistance in their respective fields operation,[25] although both the
Charter and the Specialized Agency agreements concluded with the
United Nations would seem to provide ample legal and constitutional
grounds for so doing. Furthermore, the views expressed by the United
Kingdom and United States delegates, concerning the political situation
and the economic assessment of Zambia's needs, indicate some withdrawal from previous positions. In the consultations held in London
between the Special Mission and the Minister of State of Foreign and
Commonwealth Office, the Minister is reported to have said that the
fact that Zambia had unilaterally decided to close the border was
entirely a matter for its own decision and that the closure was "Zambia's internal affair," the implication being that Zambia was estopped
from asserting an obligation on the part of the international community to render assistance. In fairness to Britain, however, it
should be pointed out that it currently provides approximately £4
million annually in technical assistance, that it has provided con-
tingency aid to Zambia since the imposition of mandatory sanctions
and is underwriting the construction of the Kariba North Power
Scheme.[26] The United States policy toward Rhodesia, when not supporting the Smith regime, is composed largely of benign neglect and
apparent indifference to the suffering of the oppressed majority and,
barring a complete reversal of priorities in Washington, holds out
little hope of assistance to a beseiged Zambia. As for the Soviet
Union, its negative attitude to collective measures is notorious, and
it has neatly resolved the problem of aid to Zambia by proclaiming
the responsibility of the United Kingdom for the entire Rhodesian
situation and its consequences.

It is too early to assess the impact of these latest events on
the Rhodesian situation. The Zambian decision to close its border
and the accompanying economic dislocation is seen as an act of
political courage by some and economic recklessness by others,
but it has produced undeniable results. It has increased pressure
on Rhodesia; it has dramatically revived the question of the effectiveness of sanctions; and it has forced the international community to
reconsider its obligations vis-à-vis adversely affected third states
and the application of new principles of international cooperation.
In the words of the Indian delegate to the Security Council, "The
resolution of the economic problems facing Zambia is directly related to the proclaimed desire of the United Nations to impose full

71

sanctions on Southern Rhodesia and to make them effective. . . .
Here then is a country which comes to us and tells us that it is determined to apply the resolutions of the United Nations and asks for
our help in reducing the difficulties it will face because of its special
geographical position and because of its past economic history and
dependence on southern Africa. It is not asking for profits, nor
quibbling about infinitely small economic burdens which other countries can easily bear. How great the burden it will have to face in
implementing fully the policy of sanctions is clear from the Special
Mission's report itself. The immediate need of nearly $150 million
seems to be about a third of the amount the Zambian government
collects as its yearly revenue. If, in these circumstances, the United
Nations, its member governments, and Specialized Agencies cannot,
according to their means, give relief to Zambia in order to overcome its present difficulties and eliminate its dependence on southern
territories, our claim that we wish to make the sanctions effective
will be totally false."[27]

NONOBSERVANCE

The statistical measurement of the effectiveness of sanctions
is derived from Rhodesia's trade figures. The most recently published
statistics released by the Security Council Sanctions Committee reveal that Rhodesian exports, after declining from $399 million in 1965
to $234 million in 1968, recovered to $379 million in 1971 and climbed
to $490 million in 1972, substantially surpassing the pre-UDI total.
By the same token, Rhodesian imports, after declining from $334
million in 1965 to $236 million in 1966, have steadily increased, par-
ticularly in 1970 and 1971, with the result that by 1972 imports totaled
$417 million, an increase of $83 million over the 1965 figure. These
figures are eloquent and disturbing proof of the degree to which the
sanctions policy has been undermined through both overt and covert
breaches of sanctions.[28]
Generally speaking, overt nonobservance of sanctions has been
of two kinds: a rejection of the sanctions policy as a whole or specific
violations, usually more or less justified on special grounds.
Only two states, South Africa and Portugal, have categorically
refused to comply with United Nations policy. As the second report
of the Security Council Sanctions Committee observed in 1969:

The governments of South Africa and Portugal have not
taken any measures to implement the provisions of
Resolution 253 (1968), have continued to maintain close
economic, trade, and other relations with the illegal

72

regime and to permit the free flow of goods from Southern Rhodesia through the territories of South Africa and the colony of Mozambique and their ports and transport facilities.[29]

The South African and Portuguese rejection of sanctions has made it possible for Rhodesia to breach sanctions on a massive scale, some measure of which may be adjudged from the fact that $330 million worth of Rhodesian exports to world markets and $233 million worth of its imports in 1972 were unaccounted for.[30] It is assumed that most of this volume transited as indirect trade through South Africa and the Portuguese-controled territories of Angola and Mozambique. This is corroborated, circumstantially at least, by the import trade statistics of South Africa, Mozambique, and Angola which have increased dramatically since 1965. In addition, South Africa, which has a much larger domestic market than the Portuguese territories, has also absorbed a considerable increase in imports from Rhodesia ($41 million worth in 1965 and $100 million in 1972).[31]

The political foundations of the policy of noncooperation by South Africa and Portugal are well known and need no rehearsal here. The problem that this poses for the international community is, in reality, only part of the larger question of how to deal with apartheid and white supremacy in southern Africa as a whole—a problem which has effectively defied solution for more than two decades. The fact is that South Africa and Portugal have for many years frustrated the United Nations with impunity not only in regard to sanctions but also in regard to gross violations of human rights in their own territories. Although a majority of United Nations members favor an extension of sanctions to both South Africa and the Portuguese territories, the necessary consensus in the Security Council is unattainable in the present political conjuncture, and the intrinsic weakness of the sanctions policy—an inability to sanction noncompliance and violations— thus persists. The enlargement of the scope of sanctions does not appear to be a realistic policy at the present time, but in the light of the Zambian border closure, the pressure for alternative methods of improving the effectiveness of sanctions and in particular measures to counterbalance South Africa and Portugal has increased.

The statistics published in the Sixth Report of the Sanctions Committee, however, also indicate a substantial degree of both overt and covert violations by "respectable" states. The extent of covert violations may be gauged by the fact that the aggregate of Rhodesian imports between 1969 and 1972 (that is, in the four years since the imposition of comprehensive mandatory sanctions), which cannot be accounted for in the trade statistics of other countries, is $701 million; the corresponding figure for Rhodesian exports is $936 million.[32]

In addition to these disguised violations, there are a number of states that have continued to trade more or less openly with Rhodesia since 1965, including Australia, Japan, the Federal Republic of Germany, and Switzerland.[33] The most recent addition to these states is the United States of America which resumed importing Rhodesian chrome ore in 1971-72. Australia maintained its pre-UDI level of exports to Rhodesia through 1971 largely on "humanitarian" grounds. The new Labor government in that country has brought this highly questionable practice to an end.

The problem in these cases is not the same as that posed by South Africa and Portugal. All of these "respectable" states consider themselves bound by the sanctions policy legally or, as in the case of Switzerland, morally, and they are, therefore, susceptible to the political pressure exerted by the Sanctions Committee which, generally speaking, has been successful in securing more adequate compliance with sanctions by states whose violations have been partial or sectorial and where it has been possible to draw the commission of violations to the attention of the government concerned. But the ability to sanction violations in legal as distinct from moral terms remains a major problem for the international community whether the violations be general or specific in nature.

NOTES

1. See First section of Chapter 10.

2. Albert Speer, Inside the Third Reich, Macmillan, London, 1970.

3. Amelia C. Leiss, ed., Apartheid and United Nations Collective Measures, an analysis, (New York: Carnegie Endowment for International Peace, 1965).

4. Ibid., p. 99.

5. At the time of writing, the Federal Republic of Germany and the German Democratic Republic are on the verge of becoming members. According to Article 4, paragraph 2, of the Charter, admission of new members is effected by a decision of the General Assembly upon the recommendation of the Security Council. The ratification of the treaty on basic relations, which entered into force on June 21, 1973, opens the way for early admission of the two Germanys to the United Nations. See Le Monde, June 10-11, 1973, p. 3.

6. Article 35, Vienna Convention on the Law of Treaties.

7. Ibid., Article 38.

8. Security Council Resolution 216.

9. See the Fifth Report of the Security Council Committee, established in pursuance of Resolution 253 (1968) concerning the

question of Southern Rhodesia (hereinafter referred to as the Sanctions Committee), United Nations Doc. S/10852, December 31, 1972, p. 21.

10. See, for example, the statement by the Zambian representative to the Security Council at its meeting on March 8, 1973. United Nations Doc. S/PV., 1692, p. 23.

11. See United Nations Doc. S/8786/Add. 2, p. 4.

12. See the Report of the Security Council Special Mission, established under Resolution 326 (1973), United Nations Doc. S/10896/Add. 1, March 6, 1973, p. 19.

13. United Nations Doc. S/10865.

14. United Nations Doc. S/PV., 1687, p. 6.

15. Ibid., pp. 14-15.

16. United Nations Doc. S/10875.

17. United Nations Doc. S/10876.

18. See the Report of the Security Council Special Mission, established under Resolution 326 (1973), United Nations Doc. S/10896.

19. United Nations Doc. S/10896/Add. 1.

20. Ibid., p. 3.

21. Ibid., pp. 3-4.

22. United Nations Doc. S/10896/Add. 1, p. 3.

23. United Nations Doc. S/10898/Rev. 1.

24. United Nations Doc. S/10899/Rev. 1.

25. See, for example, the remarks of the United States Representative Mr. Phillips in explanation of vote, United Nations Doc. S/PV., 1694, pp. 48-50.

26. The Special Mission obtained a different opinion from the Secretary-General of the Commonwealth Secretariat on the question of Zambia's closure of the border. In his view the Zambian government "very understandably, was taking the position that it could not be expected to rely, for essential imports and exports, on a route that could be opened and shut irresponsibly and without consultation." United Nations Doc. S/10896, paragraph 51.

27. Mr. Sen of India in the Security Council on March 10, 1973. See United Nations Doc. S/PV., 1694, pp. 11-12.

28. See Sixth Report of the Sanctions Committee, United Nations Doc. S/11178/Add. 2, pp. 4, 6.

29. United Nations Doc. S/9252, June 12, 1969, p. 16.

30. Sixth Report of the Sanctions Committee, loc. cit.

31. Ibid., p. 4, Table 2.

32. Ibid., Table 4 and Table 2.

33. Ibid., Appendix I and II.

10

**NATIONAL IMPLEMENTATION
OF INTERNATIONAL OBLIGATIONS:
THE DOMESTIC ENFORCEMENT
OF SECURITY COUNCIL SANCTIONS**

THE IMPLEMENTATION OF INTERNATIONAL
DECISIONS WITHIN THE STATE

We have already noted that Security Council decisions are not
directly applicable or self-executing within the jurisdiction of states.
Even though its decisions are mandatory, the Security Council is not
vested with "legislative" powers or supranational functions which,
to the extent that they exist at all in the United Nations system, are
largely confined to technical regulations in such fields as telecom-
munications, health, and meteorology. But even here, strictly speaking, it is not correct to speak of directly applicable regulations
because the Constitutions of the Specialized Agencies provide that
states may reserve the right to refuse to apply such regulations in
certain circumstances.[1] By comparison, regulatory acts stricto
senso are a feature, perhaps the most celebrated feature, of the
European Communities. Under Article 189 of the Treaty of Rome,
the Council of Ministers and the Commission of the European Communities are empowered to make regulations: "A regulation applies
generally. It is binding in all its aspects and is directly applicable
within the territories of all member states." Regulations of the
European Communities are not only mandatory for states, but may
lay down rules for individuals and enterprises within states and are
directly enforceable in municipal law. This characteristic has led
many observers to question whether European Community law is a
species of international law at all or whether it is not rather a sui
generis legal system somewhere between international law and
municipal law. Before examining the specific implementation of
sanctions by individual states, it may be useful, therefore, to say a
few words generally about the implementation of decisions of international organizations within the state.

Decisions of the Security Council under Chapter VII of the Charter are clearly decisions of an international law character, and the first question that arises in this context, therefore, is the relationship between international law and municipal law. This question constitutes one of the oldest and most celebrated of doctrinal controversies and has given rise to two schools of thought: the dualist school, which holds that the two systems are distinct, and the monist school, which holds that the two systems are united within the framework of one global legal order.

On a practical level, however, the question must be answered by reference to the position adopted by each state, which is not always as clear-cut as the doctrinal theories suggest. In the United Kingdom, for example, a distinction is made between customary international law and treaty law. Customary international law is considered to be part of the law of the land. Treaties, however, are not so considered, and such treaties as affect private rights of the individual must receive parliamentary assent through an enabling act of Parliament, that is to say, that the treaty must be incorporated into English law in order to be enforceable by English courts. Thus, although in relation to custom British practice appears to accept the monist hypothesis, as far as treaties are concerned, the dualist approach is followed. The United States, on the other hand, adheres more firmly to the monist doctrine following the English common law rule as to custom and providing in its Constitution that treaties duly concluded shall take effect as municipal law and be directly binding on individuals as well as upon the courts. Many civil law countries have adopted in their Constitutions the principle that international law is the law of the land, and some have even gone beyond the common law practice by proclaiming the supremacy of international law over municipal law.

This last point raises a question of considerable importance with respect to the enforcement of Security Council sanctions within the state. In common law countries, there is a presumption against conflicts between international and municipal law, and the corollary is that a rule of municipal law that appears to conflict with international law must always be interpreted in such a manner as to avoid such conflict. But this is not always possible, and the question must be posed as to how such a conflict may be resolved. In states where the legislature is the supreme authority, the courts must apply the law laid down for them notwithstanding that it is contradictory to rules of international law. In other words, municipal law must prevail. This is the system in Britain, according to which legislation that is incompatible with a traety must continue to be applied unless and until it is modified or abrogated by new legislation, and this is also the system in states where a treaty is regarded as having the force of municipal law such as the United States. In such jurisdictions where treaty and statute are on a basis of equality, a new treaty prevails over an earlier statute, and conversely a new statute may prevail over a treaty. Only if the Constitution provides expressly for the primacy of treaty law over municipal law, as in the case of Article 55 of the French Constitution, will a treaty prevail over subsequent as well as earlier legislation.[2] That the question is not theoretical is borne out by the recent example provided by the United States where legislative enactments subsequent to the imposition of Security Council sanctions have had the effect of countermanding certain provisions of the sanctions policy (see below, "The United States").

The position in countries that have a centrally planned economy is somewhat different. The internal measures adopted by countries with a free market economy are, of course, directed mainly to private individuals and corporations with a view to preventing them from trading or conducting any transactions with individuals and corporations in the target state. But in countries in which industry and commerce, including transport and other services, are controlled by the state, the middleman is eliminated, and the question of controlling transactions with target state is therefore reduced to one level, that of the government alone. If the government decides to comply with the measures decided upon by the Security Council, then it may be assumed that implementation by state enterprises will automatically follow so that problems of implementation are unlikely to arise.

THE UNITED KINGDOM

The United Kingdom is subject to special responsibilities and obligations in the implementation and enforcement of the sanctions policy. Security Council Resolution 253 expressly underlines this dual responsibility of the United Kingdom, which is not only bound by the terms of the comprehensive sanctions policy as set out in paragraphs 3 to 6 of the Resolution, but also by paragraph 21, which specifically requests the United Kingdom government "to give maximum assistance to the [Sanctions] Committee and to provide the Committee with any information which it may receive in order that the measures envisaged in this Resolution and Resolution 232 (1966) may be rendered fully effective." This provision reflects and confirms the primary residual responsibility of the United Kingdom, as the administering power, in achieving a solution to the Rhodesian problem.

British policy toward Rhodesia since UDI has been largely dominated by the stick, but the carrot has also made an appearance from time to time, especially and with increasing frequency since the return of a Conservative government to office in 1970. The Labor government under Harold Wilson had unsuccessfully attempted to

negotiate a settlement in 1966 and again in 1968 within the terms of
the five principles enunciated in 1964 by the then Prime Minister
Sir Alec Douglas Home:

1. unimpeded progress to majority rule;
2. guarantees against retrogressive amendment of the Constitution;
3. immediate improvement in the political status of the African
   population;
4. progress toward ending racial discrimination; and
5. the acceptability of the constitutional terms to the people of
   Rhodesia as a whole.

Then in November 1971, proposals for a settlement were agreed upon
between the Foreign Secretary Sir Alec Douglas Home and the Rhodesian Prime Minister Ian Smith. Under the terms of this agreement,
it was estimated, majority rule could be achieved at the earliest by
the year 2035, but in all probability it would be much later. The proposals established a racially segregated franchise, raised the qualifications for African voters, placed a limit of 10 on the majority that
could be attained by Africans in the lower house, and weakened procedures designed to prevent retrogressive amendments to the Constitution. The proposals were condemned by many observers, both
inside and outside Britain, as a sellout. Fortunately, however, the
principle of acceptability was retained, ironically enough it seems
upon the insistence of Ian Smith who apparently was confident that
the rural Africans were sufficiently docile and apolitical to accept
whatever "guidance" was offered to them by the district Commissioners
and government-supported Chiefs. The mission to test acceptability
of the proposals, established under the chairmanship of Lord Pierce,
was regarded as a formality by officials in Salisbury and Whitehall,
but in overwhelmingly rejecting the terms of the settlement, the
Africans in Rhodesia provided Ian Smith, the British government,
and world opinion with an example of the democratic process at work.
The Pierce Commission, therefore, had no alternative but to advise
the British government that the proposals were not acceptable to the
people of Rhodesia as a whole.

Politically then, British policy toward Rhodesia since 1965 must
be seen as increasingly ambivalent. The 1971 settlement proposals
certainly reflected a strong desire on the part of the government to
reach a negotiated settlement at almost any price and a willingness
to do so largely on the basis of the maintenance of the status quo.
This obviously conflicts with the sanctions policy which, in theory
at any rate, is maintained in order to bring an end to the rebellion
against the Crown and in order to implement the principle of self-
determination.

Despite this ambivalence, Britain has conscientiously applied sanctions since 1965 and has unquestionably been the mainstay of the Security Council Sanctions Committee. One measure of this is that of the 138 cases brought to the attention of the Committee by the end of 1972, a total of 127 had been reported by Britain.[3]

Under English law decisions of international organizations that affect individual rights and obligations and that require enforcement by English courts must receive parliamentary assent through an enabling Act of Parliament. As regards decisions of the United Nations, there is a general provision in the United Nations Act 1946 the purpose of which is to enable the government to make by Orders in Council such provisions as appear necessary or expedient to enable it to implement measures decided by the Security Council under Article 41 of the Charter. Rhodesia, of course, is something of a special case, and it was considered more expedient by the British government to enact new legislation rather than to proceed under the general provisions of the United Nations Act. The basic source of legislation with respect to the implementation of sanctions against Rhodesia is, therefore, the Southern Rhodesia Act of November 16, 1965, which recited the sovereignty of the Crown over Rhodesia and, by Section 2, subsection 2, paragraph (c), enabled the Crown by Order in Council to impose "prohibitions, restrictions, or obligations in respect of transactions relating to Southern Rhodesia." Implementation of specific measures has been primarily through the promulgation of Orders in Council subject to approval by Parliament. Parliamentary approval of the optional sanctions and mandatory selective sanctions was obtained without difficulty, but approval of mandatory comprehensive sanctions under Resolution 253 of the Security Council was achieved not without hardship.

Pursuing the normal procedure, the government sought to implement Resolution 253 through the promulgation of an Order in Council—the Southern Rhodesia (United Nations sanctions, No. 2) Order—which was approved by the Privy Council on June 7, 1968 and entered into force on June 14, 1968. Subject to the approval of Parliament within 28 days of its promulgation, the Order was approved by the House of Commons on June 16 by 319 votes to 246, but rejected by the House of Lords on June 18 by 193 votes to 184. From the practical point of view, the opposition of the House of Lords was of little consequence since the upper chamber may only delay but not prevent statutory enactments. Nevertheless, the negative vote in the House of Lords, like the tip of the iceberg, is indicative of greater danger lurking below the surface. A new Order identical to the first was made on June 28 and came into operation on July 3, 1968.

Thus, through new legislative provisions or under existing legislation, as in the case of exchange controls, the United Kingdom government has implemented the obligations incumbent upon it by virtue of Security Council Resolutions 232 and 253. This legislative action has been vigorously reinforced by judicial and administrative enforcement. Since the beginning of the mandatory sanctions in 1968, the government has obtained 11 convictions against United Kingdom companies for violations of sanctions. The earliest of these concerned a Manchester-based company (the Super Heater Co. Ltd.), which was fined a total of £27,750 plus costs for the evasion of sanctions in force under Security Council Resolution 232 by entering into 10 substitute sales contracts with agents in South Africa. The goods in question were delivered to Port Elizabeth in South Africa for transportation by rail to Bulawayo, Rhodesia. The Company pleaded not guilty.[4] In July 1968 the Lloyds and Scottish Finance Company was fined £20,010 for contravention of the Exchange Control Act of 1947, which had become applicable to Rhodesia by virtue of the Exchange Control Act (Scheduled Territories) Order of 1965. This Company had ceded to the Netherlands Bank of South Africa without Treasury permission its participation in a Rhodesian company, the Scottish-Rhodesian Finance Ltd., of which it had a controlling interest. In this case the defendants had pleaded guilty.[5] Other reported cases include a £22,000 fine imposed on a firm for exporting carpeting yarn to Rhodesia[6] and a £20,000 ($46,250) fine imposed in May 1971 for exporting goods to Rhodesia, even though most of the exports had taken place before the adoption of Security Council Resolution 253, because the exports constituted breaches of existing United Kingdom regulations covering trade with Rhodesia.[7]

Judicial enforcement has not been confined to companies, and there are a number of reported cases of fines on individuals ranging from £10 for sending electronic components to Rhodesia[8] to £325 for sending a £250 money order for payment of a debt contracted prior to UDI.[9] In addition to judicial enforcement, administrative action, especially with regard to freedom of movement of individuals, has also been employed by the British authorities.*

The effects of these measures, at least as far as trade is concerned, is that United Kingdom exports of all commodities to Rhodesia, which totaled $88,800,000 in 1965, declined to $1,796,000 in 1971 and that average exports for the five years from 1968 to 1972 were approximately $1,600,000 a year.[10] The figures for United

---

*The most esoteric example of administrative enforcement is the case of Mr. Chappel who, in April 1968 en route to a world plowing championship in Rhodesia, was prevented by British Customs authorities from taking his plow with him, plows being among the items on the prohibited exports list.

81

Kingdom imports from Rhodesia show that in 1965 the United Kingdom imported $83,711,000 worth of all commodities from Rhodesia compared with $222,000 worth in 1972. The average for the five years from 1968 to 1971 is less than $170,000 per annum.[11]

While statistically, at any rate, Britain has compiled an impressive record in fulfillment of its obligations contracted under Security Council Resolutions which, it should be remembered, are designed to enable it to restore its effective authority in Rhodesia, a certain malaise arising from an apparent ambivalence in British policy nevertheless remains. Whether by accident or design, Britain has created the impression that it is not pursuing to the maximum the opportunities available to it in the United Nations, particularly in connection with the functioning of the Sanctions Committee (see Chapter 11).

THE UNITED STATES

United States-Rhodesian trade was conducted at a very modest level prior to UDI. In 1965 total imports of the United States from Rhodesia were a little more than $14 million, while exports stood at $23 million.[12] The most important item in United States-Rhodesian trade has traditionally been chrome ore. The United States imported $5 million worth of Rhodesian chrome ore in 1965, and shipments to the United States continued at a high level through 1967.[13] Thereafter, they ceased as a consequence of Security Council Resolution 253.

The United Nations Participation Act of 1945 grants to the President of the United States authority to implement decisions of the Security Council by executive order. Until 1971 the United States complied fully with the United Nations sanctions policy, and as a consequence its imports declined sharply to $807,000 and its exports to $652,000.[14] But in 1971 a conflict arose between United States obligations under international law and domestic legislation. In November 1971, the Armed Forces Procurement Appropriations Authorization Act became law. An amendment inserted into that law, on the initiative of Senator Byrd, effectively bars the President from prohibiting the import of Rhodesian chrome and other strategically necessary materials into the United States despite the mandatory provisions of Security Council sanctions resolutions. Figures released in Washington in February 1973 reveal that in 1972 the United States had imported $13.3 million worth of chrome, nickel, and asbestos from Rhodesia, that is to say, almost three times the amount imported in 1965. At the same time, the official in charge of the United States strategic stockpiles was quoted as saying that the United States had a surplus of 2.2 million tons of chrome ore and that imports of

Rhodesian chrome were not necessary for America's national security.[15]

This overt violation of a binding decision of the Security Council is clearly and unequivocally a breach of international law and, from the point of view of domestic law, creates a legally anomalous situation whereby the government is in the position of sanctimoniously prosecuting individuals and corporations for violations of one part of the sanctions policy while at the same time actively engaged in violating another part of the same policy. Thus, for example, while the United States government was presenting to the Sanctions Committee a report on shipments of strategic materials imported into the United States from Rhodesia in the period April 1 to June 30, 1972, it also reported that indictments had been handed down by a United States Grand Jury against four individuals and two corporations in connection with an attempt to build a $50 million chemical fertilizer plant in Rhodesia and a secret agreement with the Rhodesian regime to ship $5 million worth of ammonia to Rhodesia.[16] Attempts have been made to justify the Byrd amendment on grounds of national security, but even if this did represent a ground for violation of sanctions which it does not, the justification rings somewhat hollow in the light of the admissions of government officials. That this situation of international illegality can prevail is a result of the American doctrine concerning conflicts between domestic and international law. As we observed in the section on "The Implementation of International Decisions within the State," subsequent domestic legislation may, in American practice, supersede treaty obligations, and this is precisely the effect of the Byrd amendment. This has now been reaffirmed, in the instant case, by the Supreme Court of the United States itself.

Legal action to halt the imports of Rhodesian chrome was initiated by a group of black members of Congress in 1972. The United States Court of Appeals, although finding that the law authorizing imports of Rhodesian chrome showed "blatant disregard of our treaty undertakings" as a member of the United Nations, ruled that under the Constitution Congress had the power to "set treaty obligations at naught," and the lower court therefore declined to intervene. Without commenting upon the merits of the case, the Supreme Court announced on April 16, 1973 that it would not consider an appeal.[17] The only remedy, therefore, is the repeal of the Byrd amendment by Congress.

Spokesmen for the United States government in the United Nations and elsewhere have resorted to a variety of arguments in defense of the violation of sanctions, invoking national security, respect for domestic constitutional requirements, and the argument that many other countries are engaged covertly in doing what the United States government is doing quite openly. The underlying motivations of and issues raised by the Byrd amendment have been dealt with in an excellent report[18] prepared by the United Nations Association of the United States; from the point of view of international law, however, it is sufficient to say that the United States is clearly in violation of its international obligations and that no amount of casuistic reasoning can overcome this simple fact.

The effect of the Byrd amendment on the sanctions policy cannot be measured in monetary or statistical terms alone. The most damaging consequence of the Byrd amendment is the moral and psychological encouragement that it provides to the Smith regime and the concomitant undermining of the viability of international sanctions and, indirectly, the United Nations. The Byrd amendment, therefore, represents a serious retreat from the legal and moral obligations of the United States under international law, violating the fundamental principle upon which all law is based, that agreements freely entered into are binding.

THE IMPLEMENTATION OF SECURITY COUNCIL
DECISIONS BY NONMEMBER STATES

We have already examined from the theoretical and doctrinal point of view the special problems raised by the implementation of the Security Council decisions in nonmember states. It will be useful at this juncture to examine the practice of two such states, the Federal Republic of Germany and Switzerland, because although they are both nonmembers of the United Nations, their international status is quite different and has dictated somewhat different approaches on the level of internal law.

The Federal Republic of Germany, although not yet a member of the United Nations, unilaterally declared its willingness to participate in sanctions against Rhodesia. A note verbale of April 25, 1969 addressed to the Secretary-General of the United Nations stated that "the Federal Republic of Germany has from the outset participated in the sanctions imposed on Southern Rhodesia by the Security Council since 1965, and on August 28, 1968 decided to join in the mandatory sanctions based on Security Council Resolution 253. . . ."[19] Technically, compliance with the sanctions policy in Germany was effected by two ordinances of February 14, 1967 based on a provision of the German law on foreign trade of April 28, 1961, which enables the Federal Government to restrict imports or exports on grounds of foreign policy. The constitutionality of these ordinances has been questioned by some German writers on the grounds of their generality. According to some writers, the German Constitutional Court should examine in each individual case whether a particular transaction would endanger the foreign relations of the Federal Republic.*

Whatever constitutional controversy the implementation of sanctions within the Federal Republic may have caused, the published trade statistics released by the Sanctions Committee reveal a startling discrepancy between theory and practice at least through 1968. According to its note verbale, Germany had complied with sanctions since 1965. The trade figures, however, show that between 1965 and 1968 the Federal Republic's export trade with Rhodesia actually increased from $10.9 million in 1965 to $12.9 million in 1968, while imports from Rhodesia declined substantially from $35 million in 1965 to $13.2 million in 1968.[20] For a brief period, therefore, it would seem that German exporters were able to profit from, and fill, the gap created by the embargoes enforced by other countries. However, as a result of the vigilance of the Sanctions Committee, the stricter enforcement of controls on trade appears to have taken hold in 1969, and the figures for the period 1969 to 1971 show a very considerable decrease in both the import and export of commodities into Rhodesia. German imports from Rhodesia in 1972 were a mere $367,000, although exports remained at more than $2 million.[21]

Switzerland is a member of several of the Specialized Agencies, but, as we have already pointed out above, its political neutrality has acted as a self-imposed bar on United Nations membership. As a member of the Specialized Agencies, however, Switzerland has been invited by the Security Council to participate in sanctions against Rhodesia. In a statement of February 10, 1967, the Swiss Federal Council informed the Secretary-General that for reasons of principle, Switzerland, as a neutral state, could not submit to the mandatory sanctions of the United Nations. Independently of the Security Council Resolutions, however, Switzerland agreed to limit the level of its trade with Rhodesia to the "normal" established level.[22] Following the adoption by the Security Council of Resolution 253 in May 1968, the Swiss Federal Council reiterated its previous position, additionally agreeing to ensure" . . . that Rhodesian commerce will be given no opportunity to circumvent United Nations sanctions on Swiss territory."[23] The measures taken by Switzerland to enforce this policy include the nonrecognition of Rhodesia, a prohibition on the export

---

*The author is grateful to Professor Ignaz Seidl-Hohenveldern for the information concerning the Federal Republic of Germany. Following the admission of the Federal Republic of Germany to membership of the United Nations in 1973, compliance with the Security Council sanctions became a matter of international obligation rather than unilateral choice.

of war materials to Rhodesia, and the adoption of domestic legislation designed to hold imports from Rhodesia to the normal flow of trade. Specific prohibitions on exports were not considered necessary (except for arms), because the goods specifically embargoed by the Security Council are not exported from Switzerland.[24]

In effect then, Switzerland has taken the position, which it is legally entitled to do, that it will not apply sanctions against Rhodesia as a matter of legal obligation. But what of its moral obligations to the international community of which it is a constituent member? The response, however unsatisfactory it may be, is that Switzerland will permit only the normal level of trade relations and undertake to prevent Swiss territory from being used for transshipment of goods bound to or from Rhodesia. The Sanctions Committee figures reveal that Swiss imports from Rhodesia have, in fact, been maintained at the normal level of approximately $4.5 million per annum, although the 1970 and 1971 figures register some increase over the figures for 1967, 1968, and 1969. Exports by Switzerland to Rhodesia have steadily increased from $1.6 million in 1965 to $3.2 million in 1972. Between 1969 and 1972, in particular, there has taken place a quantum twofold increase in the value of Swiss exports to Rhodesia.[25]

The primary concern of the Sanctions Committee, however, is with the transshipment opportunities afforded by Swiss law, and although the Swiss authorities have undertaken to prevent this kind of activity, no specific information is available on what measures, if any, have been taken by the federal authorities. Admittedly, the problems to be encountered in controlling such activities may be very complex as the Universal Exports Ltd. (UNIVEX) affair illustrates.

In February 1969 the United Kingdom government received reliable information that the Rhodesian regime had formed UNIVEX, a state enterprise, expressly for the purpose of coordinating the evasion of sanctions. UNIVEX, in conjunction with a South African firm Arnold Wilhelmy & Co. of Johannesburg, controlled a Zurich firm Handelsgesellschaft which, in turn, coordinated the sale of Rhodesian chrome ores and alloys in Europe and supervised the activities of sales agents in various European countries.

By routing shipments of chrome ore through Lourenco Marques in Mozambique, falsifying certificates of origin and using as an intermediary a legitimate registered corporation in Switzerland, UNIVEX was believed to have handled the export of some 10,000 tons of Rhodesian chrome ore and ferrochrome over a 10-month period in 1968 and 1969.[26]

A more recent case illustrates how the Federal Republic of Germany and Switzerland may be used by legitimate enterprises to evade sanctions. It was reported on April 17, 1973 that three Boeing jet aircraft had been delivered to Rhodesia despite the economic blockade. The three jets had been owned by a bankrupt West German charter company, Calair of Munich, and had subsequently been sold to a company registered in Lichtenstein. They were prepared for a flight to Lisbon, Portugal, by Jet Aviation an aircraft maintenance company in Basle, Switzerland.[27] From Lisbon the jets were flown to Salisbury, Rhodesia. This case provides an excellent illustration of how "informal" compliance with Security Council Resolutions may lead to the subversion of United Nations policy and why it is absolutely essential that blind spots in the sanctions net be closed. The West German transaction, whereby the jets were sold to a Lichtenstein-registered company, was undoubtedly a lawful transaction according to both German and Lichtenstein law. The Lichtenstein company entered into an agreement with unidentified "Portuguese" interests for sale of the aircraft presumably to a dummy corporation acting on behalf of Rhodesia. The Swiss authorities, on whose territory the aircraft were made ready for the flight to Lisbon, no doubt acted on the basis of papers showing the destination of the jets to be Lisbon. Security Council Resolution 253 expressly enjoins the members of the United Nations from allowing their territories to be used for transactions of this kind with Rhodesia.[28] The circumstances of the sale and the Lisbon destination would, at the very least, have warranted an investigation on the part of Swiss authorities as to the ultimate destination of the aircraft in order to ensure that Swiss territory was not being used to circumvent sanctions.

The consequence of the admission of the Federal Republic of Germany to the United Nations is that Germany will henceforth be bound by the relevant Security Council Resolutions on a mandatory rather than a voluntary basis. A tightening of Swiss policy on sanctions would also be highly desirable. As long as Rhodesia can provide the foreign exchange for such transactions and as long as loopholes of the Swiss or German variety exist, the international sanctions policy will be in jeopardy.

NOTES

1. See, for example, Article 10 of the Constitution of the World Health Organization and Article 8 of the World Meteorological Organization.

2. Resolution 253 was given effect in France by a decree of August 23, 1968. See Journal Official, August 27, 1968, p. 8215.

3. See the Fifth Report of the Sanctions Committee, United Nations Doc. S/10852/Add. 1, pp. 3-12. As of December 15, 1973, the number of cases under active consideration by the Committee totaled 172. See the Sixth Report of the Sanctions Committee, United Nations Doc. S/11178/Add. 2, p. 3.

4. The Times (London), January 11, 1968.

5. Ibid., July 20, 1968.

6. See the Fourth Report of the Sanctions Committee, United Nations Doc. S/10229, paragraph 38, p. 12.

7. See the Fifth Report of the Sanctions Committee, loc. cit., paragraph 47, p. 12.

8. Fourth Report of the Sanctions Committee, loc. cit.

9. Ibid., paragraph 36.

10. Sixth Report of the Sanctions Committee, loc. cit., Appendix II.

11. Ibid., Appendix I.

12. Ibid.

13. Ibid., paragraph 15, p. 10.

14. Ibid., Appendixes I and II.

15. The Economist, February 1973.

16. United Nations Doc. S/10852/Add. 1, Annex I, p. 6.

17. The New York Times, April 17, 1973.

18. "Rhodesian Chrome." A research report by the Washington Intern Program of the Student and Young Adult Division, United Nations Association of the U.S.A., 1973, 96 pages.

19. See the Second Report of the Sanctions Committee, May 29, 1968, United Nations Doc. S/9252, Annex III.

20. Fifth Report of the Sanctions Committee, loc. cit., Appendixes I and II.

21. Sixth Report of the Sanctions Committee, loc. cit., Appendixes I and II.

22. For the text of the official statement of the Swiss government, see United Nations Doc. S/7781, Annex II.

23. Fourth Report of the Sanctions Committee, loc. cit., p. 15, paragraph 52.

24. See Annuaire Suisse de Droit international, vol. XXV, 1968, p. 278.

25. Sixth Report of the Sanctions Committee, loc. cit., Appendixes I and II.

26. See, for example, the "Catharina Oldendorff" case, reported in United Nations Doc. S/9252, Annex II.

27. The Times (London), April 17, 1973.

28. See, in particular, operative paragraphs 3, 8, and 9 of Resolution 253.

11

TOWARD THE ESTABLISHMENT
OF EFFECTIVE
INTERNATIONAL MACHINERY

Must one conclude that economic sanctions organized on
a cooperative basis are doomed to failure? Not necessarily. But it certainly seems that the obstacles in their
way are gigantic—particularly if they are not supplemented
by military sanctions or, at least, by a known willingness
to use military sanctions if necessary.

The real key to the successful application of sanctions is loyal and vigorous leadership by the great powers
applying them plus a determination to make them succeed.
Otherwise there is no hope of obtaining and retaining the
essential cooperation of the lesser powers and of bringing
the aggressor to terms.[1]

These observations, apropos of the sanctions applied against
Italy between October 1935 and July 1936 under the aegis of the League
of Nations, might serve to characterize with equal validity the sanctions against Rhodesia. Certainly, insofar as the role of the great
powers is concerned, it seems clear that today, just as 35 years ago,
the attitude of the great powers will be a decisive influence in the
success or failure of the sanctions policy. Beyond this, however,
comparisons between the 1935 sanctions and Rhodesian sanctions are
not particularly helpful and can offer few reliable pointers in the
present context. To mention only two of the most obvious differences
between the past and the present, although the balance of power remains a function of a very small number of states, the considerable
expansion of the international community since 1935 has qualitatively
modified the international system within which the great powers must
function, and secondly, there are significant differences in regard to
collective security between the League and the United Nations systems.
The League of Nations was characterized by a virtually complete

decentralization of the procedure for the application of enforcement measures, whereas under the Charter of the United Nations, both the decision as to whether there exists a threat to the peace and the decision as to the application of enforcement measures are centralized within the Security Council. But even though the Charter system represents an advancement over the League of Nations, this is not as complete as the language of the Charter suggests at first sight. It is true that the Security Council's responsibility extends to the maintenance of peace and security overall and that under Chapter VII the Council is authorized to take binding decisions with regard to any threat to the peace, breach of the peace, or act of aggression. At the same time, however, there are two important limitations on the exercise of this collective security system. The first of these is inherent in the Charter system itself and relates to the voting procedures of the Security Council. Any decision of the Council under Chapter VII requires the concurring votes of the five permanent members which, translated into practical terms, means that collective measures cannot be applied against China, France, the Soviet Union, the United Kingdom, or the United States or, it should be added, any client state of the five. The second limitation stems from the nature of the international system which, despite organizational efforts to the contrary, remains stubbornly fragmented and decentralized in the political sphere. Thus, even though the first of these limitations may be overcome in a particular conjuncture, as in the case of Rhodesia, the second limiting factor remains to determine the manner in which internationally agreed sanctions are implemented by domestic agencies. The United Nations, in such circumstances, can exercise only the most limited degree of control and lacks a truly sanctionative authority. Disposing, therefore, of only the most rudimentary and inchoate machinery for the enforcement of its decisions, the Security Council nevertheless launched the United Nations on a trial of strength with Rhodesia. Successful prosecution of the policy of sanctions will strengthen the moral and legal authority of the United Nations; failure will underscore the marginality of the organization in the political sphere and seriously impair its credibility vis-à-vis the third world, possibly the United Nations' last constituency. Viewed then in relation to the importance of this particular policy to the future of the organization, the development of appropriate machinery for the supervision and control of sanctions assumes an importance possibly transcendental in nature.

The historical experience is hardly encouraging. Collective economic measures on the international or regional levels have rarely produced the desired results and have, in fact, frequently proved dysfunctional. This was the case, for example, of the sanctions against Italy in 1935-36, the collapse of which in a few short months exposed the fragility of the collective security system at that time and inadvertently strengthened Mussolini's domestic political control. Regional collective enforcement measures in the inter-American context have been equally inconclusive. The sanctions imposed on the Dominican Republic in 1960-62 were lifted following the assassination of Trujillo and before any conclusions as to their real effectiveness could be established. The blockade of Cuba, which has been in effect since 1962, has patently failed to achieve its primary political objectives and has undoubtedly helped to consolidate the authority of Fidel Castro. What evidence there is then points to the fact that economic sanctions applied in peacetime conditions are not the most effective instrument of change.

THE CREATION OF THE SANCTIONS COMMITTEE

The sense of cautious deliberation, which has characterized the formulation of the sanctions policy itself, has also featured in the creation of international machinery. In the first phase of sanctions, under Resolution 217, no provision was made concerning the coordination of information from states or other sources. With the imposition of selective mandatory sanctions in December 1966, however, it became necessary to provide for some means whereby the implementation of the Security Council's decisions could be monitored. Resolution 232, therefore, called upon member states of the United Nations or of the Specialized Agencies "to report to the Secretary-General the measures each has taken" to implement the Resolution.[2] Reporting was not mandatory, however, and the Secretary-General's periodic submissions to the Security Council throughout 1967 depicted a very uneven response from member states.[3]

The creation of the Security Council Sanctions Committee stems from the decision in May 1968 to introduce comprehensive mandatory sanctions. Paragraph 20 of Resolution 253 of May 29, 1968 established a Committee of the Security Council:

(a) To examine such reports on the implementation of the present resolution as are submitted by the Secretary-General;
(b) To seek from any States Members of the United Nations or of the Specialized Agencies such further information regarding the trade of that State (including information regarding the commodities and products exempted from the prohibition contained in operative paragraph 3 (d) above) or regarding any activities by any nationals of that State or in its territories that may constitute an

91

evasion of the measures decided upon in this resolution
as it may consider necessary for the proper discharge
of its duty to report to the Security Council.[4]

The creation of the Sanctions Committee did not immediately
diminish the incidence of violations of sanctions, but by monitoring
Rhodesian trade more closely, it provided the Security Council and
the United Nations as a whole with a relatively well-informed view
of the effectiveness or the lack of effectiveness of the measures in
force. Furthermore, the submission of Sanctions Committee reports,
though couched in appropriate diplomatic language, made it possible
to publicly identify the principal transgressors. In 1970, undoubtedly
in response to the information conveyed in these reports, the Security
Council expanded the mandate of the Sanctions Committee. By Resolution 277 of March 18, 1970, the Sanctions Committee was asked to
study "ways and means by which member states could carry out more
effectively the decisions of the Security Council regarding sanctions."[5]
Almost exactly two years later, in Resolution 314 of February 28,
1972, the Security Council again requested the Committee "to meet
as a matter of urgency to consider ways and means by which implementation of sanctions may be ensured and to submit to the Security
Council . . . a report containing recommendations in this respect,
including any suggestions which the Committee might wish to make
concerning its terms of reference and any other measures designed
to ensure the effectiveness of its work. . . ."[6]
The urgency of this latter request was prompted by a rapidly
deteriorating situation. The Fourth Report of the Sanctions Committee
published in June 1971 had indicated an unabated violation of sanctions
with respect to a wide variety of commodities including minerals,
maize, cottonseed, wheat, meat, sugar, and fertilizers.[7] The Report
contained information on a number of transactions conducted with the
consent of reporting governments, including five shipments of Rhodesian graphite imported by the Federal Republic of Germany,[8] a
shipment of meat imported by Switzerland,[9] and considerable shipments of Australian wheat to Rhodesia "in special humanitarian circumstances,"[10] all of which suggested that sanctions were being
observed with decreasing effectiveness by a growing number of governments. The passage of the Byrd amendment in September 1971 merely
seemed to confirm this tendency. The political conjuncture in the
latter part of 1971 then was, from the point of view of proponents of
sanctions, almost wholly negative. The Sanctions Committee's reports
revealed widespread violations both overt and covert; the United States
government had remained passive throughout the passage of the Byrd
amendment; and, in November 1971, the British Foreign Secretary
and the Rhodesian Prime Minister had reached agreement on proposals

for a settlement which would have entrenched white minority rule for the foreseeable future. The unexpectedly firm rejection of the proposals by the African majority and the emergence of the African National Council as an organized political force in Rhodesia, however, dramatically checked this insidious drift toward accommodation with the Smith regime. Instead of the expected adulteration of sanctions, existing sanctions have been maintained, and the Security Council, after much hesitation, has actively resumed consideration of measures to increase their effectiveness.

The Sanctions Committee meets in closed sessions, but from its well-documented published reports, it is possible to outline the procedures presently followed by the Committee. A recently reported case may be used in illustration.[11]

On March 31, 1971, the United Kingdom conveyed to the Sanctions Committee information obtained from reliable commercial sources concerning a large consignment of minerals suspected to have been mined in Rhodesia. According to the United Kingdom's information, several thousand tons of chrome ores and concentrates had been loaded at the Mozambique port of Lourenco Marques aboard the West German vessel Rotenfels for carriage to Rotterdam in the Netherlands. The vessel left Lourenco Marques on March 15 and was expected in Rotterdam on April 10. The United Kingdom government suggested that the information be relayed by the Secretary-General to the governments of the Netherlands and the Federal Republic of Germany to enable them to investigate the origin and final destination of the consignment of minerals. Following consultations within the Sanctions Committee, the Secretary-General addressed notes verbale to the governments concerned. The Dutch government replied on July 1, 1971, stating that the Rotenfels had arrived at Rotterdam on April 10 carrying a cargo of chrome ores declared for transit to the Federal Republic of Germany and Sweden. It offered to supply the Secretary-General with supplementary information concerning the data and mode of transit through the Netherlands of the consignment. At the Sanctions Committee's request, the Secretary-General conveyed the information received from the Dutch government to the West German and Swedish governments. In subsequent communications to the Secretary-General, both governments confirmed that examination of the documentation pertaining to the shipment of chrome showed the consignment to have originated in South Africa. The case was thereupon closed.

The Rotenfels case is typical of many of the cases dealt with by the Sanctions Committee both in its development and final disposition. It also illuminates the limitations of the existing procedures. A first observation to be made is that the Sanctions Committee functions on what may be termed the bureaucratic rather than the operational level. Essentially, its authority is restricted to that of receiving, analyzing, and disseminating information, while lacking any power of verification or inspection in situ. Secondly, it must rely exclusively on the voluntary submission of information from governments or intergovernmental sources. In practice, this information base has been extremely narrow. The United Kingdom has provided the overwhelming bulk of the information reaching the Sanctions Committee. Of the 138 cases of suspected violations of sanctions reported up to December 31, 1972, information on 127 cases was provided by the United Kingdom. The Sanctions Committee has been unable to develop independent sources of information, and the assistance of intergovernmental organizations and the United Nations system in general appears to have been nonexistent. Thirdly, since the Sanctions Committee pursues suspected violations through a diplomatic exchange of notes, the very nature of this procedure tends to diffuse the urgency with which the investigation should be carried out. The bureaucratization of the investigation is increased by the fact that, in many cases, several governments may be involved in different stages of the transaction, and an exchange of notes must be carried out with each government. Frequently a vessel may be registered in one country, owned or leased by a corporation in a second country, and the consignment may be destined to a third country for transshipment to a fourth and fifth country. Thus, even though time limits are established for replies to inquiries made by the Secretary-General which, in theory, are designed to limit delays to a maximum of four months, between the time when an initial inquiry is addressed to a government and the time when the Sanctions Committee may take whatever steps to ensure compliance with its request that it deems necessary, in practice once an exchange of notes has been initiated between a government and the United Nations, a considerable period of time may elapse before all the necessary information is supplied. Fourthly, the Sanctions Committee must accept a government's findings as final. For example, whereas in the majority of cases the government is requested to carry out an investigation into the origin of certain commodities, if an examination of the available documents by the government results in a finding that the commodity in question originated in South Africa or Mozambique, this must be accepted by the Sanctions Committee even though the weight of the circumstantial evidence indicates otherwise. The Sanctions Committee has no powers to inspect cargoes in situ or to compel governments to carry out expert analyses which, in the case of certain mineral commodities, may be used to determine their exact origin. Finally, even where a violation of sanctions can be conclusively demonstrated, the Sanctions Committee is competent to merely draw the matter to the attention of the Security Council. The question of what further action, if any, may be taken against the individuals, companies, or state enterprises concerned within the particular jurisdiction becomes at this point a "political" question. The obvious deficiencies of the present methods of enforcement of sanctions, as revealed by the Sanctions Committee's own reports, prompted the Security Council's two requests to the Committee to devise measures of improvement. Despite the urgency of the task, some two years elapsed before any serious undertaking occurred, surely a measure not of the bureaucratic inefficiency of the secretariat but rather of the political sensitivity of the enterprise. This latter quality is confirmed by the contents of the two Special Reports prepared by the Sanctions Committee setting forth a comprehensive series of measures.[12] While these Special Reports reflect broad agreement among the members of the Security Council on the desirability of and necessity for a more effective implementation of sanctions, they also reveal a wide disagreement concerning the precise strategy to be adopted.

A scrutiny of the Special Reports reveals two distinct approaches. The "radical" approach, adopted by the African states with the support of the Soviet Union, China, and most Third World countries, would seek to reinforce the existing measures applied to Rhodesia while at the same time extending sanctions to South Africa and the Portuguese territories of Angola and Mozambique. The moderate approach, on the other hand, preferred by the United Kingdom with the support of the United States, holds that existing procedures are adequate, that what is lacking is the political will to implement these procedures, and that consequently until existing measures function effectively it is useless to add new measures. It is greatly to the credit of the Sanctions Committee that it succeeded, to a considerable extent, in reconciling two such divergent tendencies. Although the compromise reached by the Committee tends to be less than precise in regard to some of the major demands of the African states, a comparison of the conclusions reached in the First and Second Special Reports, and particularly the depth of the political support for these conclusions, is eloquent testimony to the influence of the Committee.

The most important political development in the Committee between May 1972 and April 1973 (the dates of submission of the First and Second Reports) was the change in the attitude of the United Kingdom. Whereas the United Kingdom entered a blanket reservation to the recommendations and suggestions contained in the First Report even though they were, for the most part, either quite innocuous or rhetorical, it has accepted all the recommendations and suggestions contained in the Second Report. In conjunction with this political evolution, the Second Report also registers a marked substantive improvement. With few exceptions, the First Report contained recommendations and suggestions which were either procedural in nature (for example, changing the name of the Sanctions Committee, establishing time limits for governmental replies) or rhetorical (for example, calling on member states to implement sanctions more effectively). The Second Report, on the other hand, is replete with practical suggestions.

THE STRENGTHENING OF THE SANCTIONS COMMITTEE

The three African members of the Committee—Guinea, Kenya, and the Sudan—played a prominent role in formulating the proposals that shaped the final recommendations and suggestions contained in the Second Report. Although proposals were also submitted by other delegations, the principal basis of discussion was a 24-point working paper entitled "Proposals on the Implementation of Operative Paragraphs 4 and 5 of Security Council Resolution 320 (1972)" submitted to the Committee on February 8, 1973 on behalf of the three African delegations by the representative of the Sudan.[13]

As revealed in Parts IV and V of the Second Special Report, the tripartite proposals differed from earlier African initiatives by the extent to which they eschewed an emotional or politically unrealistic approach, typified by the rhetorical demands for sanctions against South Africa and Portugal, in favor of a practical, even businesslike, approach to the problem at hand. Thus, even though the very first proposal recommends what amounts to a quantitative embargo on selected South African, Mozambican, and Angolan commodities, the tripartite proposals nowhere suggest the establishment of a general embargo on these territories. Instead, realistically, the three African states have addressed themselves to what they perceive to be the principal weaknesses of existing procedures as revealed, in particular, by the Sanctions Committee reports. These may be identified as the inadequate or inefficient implementation of sanctions by many governments, the use of alternative trade routes through South Africa, Mozambique, and Angola, and the widespread utilization of false documents of origin.

The proposed countermeasures to combat these strategies and handicaps fall into five main groups: firstly, measures directed specifically toward South Africa, Mozambique, and Angola; secondly, measures directed specifically toward Rhodesia; thirdly, measures to elicit more adequate information concerning suspected violations of sanctions; fourthly, measures to improve the effectiveness of the national implementation of sanctions; and fifthly, measures to increase the powers and enhance the authority of the international machinery for the supervision of implementation of sanctions. It is an indication of the persuasiveness of the tripartite proposals that about half of them were finally adopted, including virtually all of those concerning information and national implementation and some of the measures designed to improve international supervision. It must be acknowledged, however, that the proposals to increase pressure directly on Rhodesia or on South Africa and the Portuguese territories did not, for the most part, meet with approval. The most significant new measures deriving from the proposals and upon which the Sanctions Committee reached agreement concern the mechanics and machinery of enforcement both national and international.

Manual of Procedures

The African delegations proposed that the Sanctions Committee should produce a manual establishing guidelines regarding the freezing, examination, and seizure of cargoes of suspected Rhodesian origin. This proposal was linked to a recommendation that all states be requested to freeze cargoes of commodities produced by Rhodesia but which are also produced by South Africa, Mozambique, or Angola, and that such cargoes should be frozen until strict identification tests had been carried out in view of the fact that the Security Council has already recognized such cargoes to be prima facie suspect.[14] The proposal has been partially adopted by the Sanctions Committee, but in a less categorical manner. The Sanctions Committee recommended that states institute procedures at the point of importation to ensure that such goods are not cleared through Customs until they are satisfied that the documentation is adequate and complete and to ensure that such procedures provide for the recall of cleared goods to Customs custody if subsequently established to be of Rhodesian origin. These measures, it is true, are something less than automatic freezing and seizure, but would nevertheless be susceptible to such implementation if a state so desired. The Sanctions Committee did adopt, however, the tripartite proposal concerning a manual of procedures. It recommended that such a manual be prepared urgently and that it should contain documentation and clearing procedures necessary to determine the true origin of products known to be produced in Rhodesia, particularly chrome ore, asbestos, tobacco, pig iron, copper, sugar, maize, and meat products and that it should also contain guidelines for confiscation in appropriate cases.[15]

Experts

The African delegations proposed the formation of a body of experts to be available at short notice for the examination and analysis of suspect cargoes with a view to the determination of the origin of the commodity. This proposal has been endorsed by the Sanctions Committee, which recommends that the Committee publish a list of experts whose names will have been provided by governments and who will be "on call" at short notice, with the consent of their governments in the case of government employers, on behalf of the government of any importing country, which will normally bear the expenses, to make an appropriate investigation. The Committee may also offer to any government of an importing country the assistance of one or more experts to investigate cargo on the spot.[16] While this recommendation is a theoretical improvement over existing procedures, in practice the employment of experts in situ is unlikely to increase on the basis of such a generally worded recommendation.

Sanctions Fund

One of the more unusual proposals advanced by the African states was that the United Nations should offer rewards for information from individuals and nongovernmental organizations leading to the discovery of violations of sanctions. This proposal presupposes the existence of a fund which, according to the working paper, could be established on the basis of proceeds from the sale of seized embargoed goods. Such goods would be sold, and after deducting necessary expenses, the proceeds would be handed over to the United Nations, which would then establish a special sanctions fund that could be used for carrying out various activities of the Sanctions Committee. The Sanctions Committee accepted these proposals and has recommended that all member states seize—in accordance with their domestic regulations, especially those based on relevant Security Council Resolutions—cargoes established to be of Rhodesian origin that have been imported or have arrived for importation into their country. It further recommends that there be established a special fund to be financed by voluntary contributions, especially the proceeds of the sales of goods seized by the states. This fund should be used for the payment of expenses of experts as well as appropriations for the other purposes consistent with Resolution 253 of 1968.[17] Although the number of cargoes seized in the past five years has been infinitesimally small [18] and, therefore, the size of the fund proposed would be of a corresponding dimension, the recommendations for establishing a group of experts coupled with the recommendation for a special sanctions fund do presage the creation of international machinery with independent financing, which would be a breakthrough of considerable significance not only for the implementation of sanctions but also in the wider context of the evolution of international organizations. Indeed, should the financing be adequate, the expertise available to the Sanctions Committee would be on a par with that which is commercially available to multi-national corporations and governments.

Appointment of a Commissioner for Sanctions

The African delegations also advanced proposals for the appointment of a Commissioner for United Nations sanctions against Rhodesia directly responsible to the Security Council and with a broad mandate to coordinate all existing action under Security Council sanctions resolutions. The Commissioner will give publicity to breaches and evasions of sanctions and to make representations to governments concerned, as well as to consider, encourage, and initiate proposals, making Security Council sanctions more effective and, where necessary, to make recommendations to the Security Council for further actions or additional authority. He is to prepare the plan of action accordingly and to report every two months to the Committee on actions taken and new recommendations for the future and to assume responsibility and leadership in positive action to achieve the purposes approved and authorized by the Security Council.

The Sanctions Committee stopped short of recommending the appointment of a Commissioner, but it did propose that the unit responsible within the Secretariat for the Sanctions Committees should be reinforced by the appointment of an "individual with experience of international commerce, particularly of trade conducted through third parties, who would be responsible to the Committee, attend all meetings of the Committee, take any necessary action including publicity action, at the Committee's request, make suggestions to the Committee and prepare work for the Committee, including, where appropriate, the submission to it of draft notes to governments requesting further clarification or explanation."[19]

The substance of the tripartite proposal then has been approved, even though there has been no agreement on the form. The appointment of a Commissioner could have a potentially significant impact on the implementation of sanctions. Experience in a number of different fields has shown that the appointment of an individual at the head of a United Nations agency may revolutionize a bureaucracy, reduce red tape, and stimulate innovative procedures. A number of such examples spring to mind: Paul Hoffman's leadership of the United Nations Development Program, Raul Prebisch at the head of the Economic Commission for Latin America, and, subsequently, UNCTAD and, more recently, Maurice Strong's direction of the United Nations Environment Program. An imaginative and dynamic Sanctions Commissioner could provide the sanctions policy with an image especially in the public information field and could adopt a far more aggressive attitude toward governments and multinational corporations than is possible for either the Secretary-General or the Sanctions Committee.

Equally instructive from the point of view of the long-term evolution of the situation are the proposals that failed to obtain approval or upon which disagreement was registered. The most important of these measures concerns the extension of sanctions to South Africa and the Portuguese territories. The tripartite working paper proposed that the Security Council should decide that all states should limit their purchases of chrome ores, asbestos, tobacco, pig iron, copper, sugar, maize, and meat products from South Africa, Mozambique, and Angola to the quantitative levels prevailing in 1965.[20] The commodities are all exported by Rhodesia, and the quantitative restriction on purchases of such commodities from South Africa, Mozambique, and Angola is an attempt to ensure that like commodities of Rhodesian origin are not "laundered" in South Africa and the Portuguese territories. Since the Sanctions Committee reports provide overwhelming circumstantial evidence that many of these commodities are funneled from Rhodesia through South Africa and the Portuguese territories, this proposal, if adopted, would block one of the principal gaps in the sanctions net. The tripartite proposal, it should be added, does not go as far as some of the alternative proposals put forward by the Soviet Union or China. The Soviet Union specifically proposed that the Council decide that all states should cease all purchases from South Africa and the Portuguese territories of commodities also produced in Rhodesia, that the Sanctions Committee should recommend to the Security Council an obligatory embargo on the sale to South Africa and Portugal of petroleum and petroleum products as well as on the delivery of arms, military equipment, material, and munitions.[21] While China refrained from proposing any specific measures, the Chinese delegation expressed its support for the expansion of sanctions to South Africa and Portugal and viewed the three-power proposals as preliminary measures.[22]

The Soviet Union is also a proponent of supplemental measures under Article 41 of the Charter, which authorizes the Security Council to sever rail, sea, air, postal, telegraphic, radio, and other means of communication.[23] One such measure was, in fact, contained in the tripartite working paper, which proposed that all states deny landing rights to the national carriers of countries that continue to grant landing rights to aircraft from Rhodesia or that operate air services to Rhodesia.[24] This proposal did not survive the Sanctions Committee debates.

The tripartite working paper also contained a series of proposals with a view to introducing restrictions in sales contracts, purchase contracts, and insurance contracts in order to either increase the risk to the carrier or create impediments to the carriage of goods by sea or air to or from Rhodesia.[25] In connection with these proposals, the Sanctions Committee interviewed Mr. Carl McDowell, President of the American Institute of Underwriters, and Mr. Roy Leifflen, who appeared as an expert consultant regarding the question of marine insurance. On the basis of the information obtained from these experts, the African delegations formed the view that their proposals were realistic and necessary, that the action envisaged would be possible, and that if implemented would make an important contribution to the effectiveness of sanctions.[26] Significantly, however, none of these proposals was approved by the Santions Committee as a whole. Instead, the United Kingdom recommended that governments be requested to discuss with their importers and exporters effective and practical precautionary steps that could be taken in order to achieve more effective application of sanctions.[27] Finally, the tripartite working paper proposed an extension of the Beira blockade to cover commodities and products originating from Rhodesia.[28] The Beira blockade, which is secured by the Royal Navy in accordance with Security Council Resolution 217, is limited to the importation by Rhodesia of petroleum and petroleum products. The Sanctions Committee could not agree on this proposal or even on a recommendation that the Security Council should inquire from member states whether they would be willing to join with the Royal Navy in patrolling the Beira Straits.

The positions adopted by various delegations in the Sanctions Committee on the basis of an examination of the Second Special Report reveal an incipient disintegration in the traditional alignment within the Security Council. The African position, presented in the Sanctions Committee by Guinea, Kenya, and the Sudan, was comprehensively supported by China, the Soviet Union, Panama, Peru, India, Indonesia, and Yugoslavia.[29] In addition, two states normally associated with the Western European or Commonwealth blocs, Austria and Australia, detached themselves explicitly from the United Kingdom's position.[30] In particular, the delegation of Australia stated that it would have been able to support more of the African proposals than had been adopted and that it would have liked to see some of the proposals that had been adopted put in a stronger form. The Austrian delegation also declared that it agreed with the intent and the spirit of the African proposal as a whole and that it could have supported a number of those proposals on which there was no agreement in the Committee, either in their original form or with minor modifications that would not have derogated from their objectives.[31] The change in attitude of Australia, which is directly attributable to a change in government, is particularly significant since Australia had been one of the more important trading partners of Rhodesia since UDI. The French position also appears

to have undergone some modification. Until quite recently, France
has been notable for its uncompromising view of the impropriety of
United Nations involvement in a "domestic" affair, and while officially
meeting the obligations deriving from the Security Council Resolutions,
the implementation of sanctions by France has been ambivalent. In
regard to the recommendations contained in the Second Special Report
of the Sanctions Committee, however, the delegation of France stated
that it was in favor of the recommendations to the extent to which
they increased the effectiveness of sanctions. With regard to the
proposals on which no agreement had been reached in the Sanctions
Committee, France nevertheless observed that it had no objections
of principle concerning four of the proposals, two which refer to
insurance clauses, one which requested the United States to cooperate
fully with the United Nations in the effective implementation of sanctions and to revoke its existing legislation permitting the importation
of minerals from Rhodesia, and one which would call upon all member
states to inform the United Nations as to their present sources of
supply for commodities that had been obtained from Rhodesia prior
to the application of sanctions.[32]

The new alignment in the Security Council Sanctions Committee,
therefore, effectively isolates the United Kingdom and the United States
as the only members basically in favor of maintaining the status quo
on sanctions.

THE LIMITS OF UNITED NATIONS ACTION

Not unexpectedly, the debate in the Security Council reflected
the positions adopted in the Sanctions Committee itself.

Guinea, Kenya, and the Sudan sponsored two draft resolutions
based on the agreed recommendations and suggestions contained in
the Second Special Report as well as a number of the nonagreed proposals. The first of these draft resolutions was eventually co-sponsored by nine states: Australia, Guinea, Kenya, India, Indonesia,
Panama, Peru, Sudan, and Yugoslavia. This registered the approval
of the Security Council of the recommendations and suggestions contained in Part III of the Second Special Report and requested the Sanctions Committee, governments, and the Secretary-General to take
urgent action to implement the recommendations. The draft resolution,
however, also embodied a number of proposals on which no agreement
had been reached in the Sanctions Committee, particularly those pertaining to purchase or sales contracts and insurance and which, in
the final vote, provoked the abstention of France, the United Kingdom,
and the United States. The resolution was adopted, however, by 12
votes to nothing with 3 abstentions.[33] A second draft resolution,

submitted by Guinea, Kenya, and the Sudan and subsequently co-sponsored by Indonesia, Panama, Peru, and Yugoslavia, would have limited the purchase of certain commodities from South Africa, Mozambique, and Angola to the quantitative level prevailing in 1965, would have decided to extend the Beira blockade to cover all commodities from or to Rhodesia through the port of Lourenco Marques, and would have requested states to take measures to deny or revoke landing rights to national carriers of countries servicing Rhodesia by air.[34] This resolution was supported by 11 members of the Security Council but failed to adoption because of the negative vote of two permanent members of the Council—the United Kingdom and the United States. Austria and France abstained.

The adoption of Resolution 333 by the Security Council on May 22, 1973 must be seen, therefore, as a mitigated success for the tripartite initiative. On the positive side, it succeeded in obtaining Security Council approval of all the recommendations and suggestions contained in the Second Special Report as well as a number of proposals that had not been agreed to in the Sanctions Committee. Thus, despite the abstention of three permanent members of the Security Council, these measures undoubtedly constitute an improvement on the existing procedures. In particular, a number of recommendations, which strengthen the international machinery, have been adopted. These include the preparation of a manual for documentation and clearing procedures and containing the guidelines for confiscation in appropriate cases, the publication of a list of experts and granting of authority to the Sanctions Committee to offer expert assistance in situ, the establishment or a special fund and the appointment of an international commercial expert to, and the strengthening of, the Committee. In addition, several other provisions of the Resolution concerning contracts of insurance provide further groundwork for an examination of commercial procedures by the Sanctions Committee.

On the negative side, the use of the veto by the United Kingdom and the United States with regard to the draft resolution contained in Document S/10928 is indicative of the limits of the sanctions policy in general, but this is something to which we shall return in our conclusions. Insofar as international machinery is concerned, the Rhodesian situation once again appears to have performed an important catalytic function by permitting the Security Council to continue and develop a dialogue which flows from the consequences of having invoked Chapter VII of the Charter.

NOTES

1. Albert E. Highley, "The First Sanctions Experiment" (A Study of League Procedures), Geneva Research Center, Geneva Studies, Vol. IX, No. 4, July 1938, p. 127.

2. Security Council Resolution 232 (1966), paragraph 8.

3. See the First Report of the Sanctions Committee, December 30, 1968, United Nations Doc. S/8954.

4. Security Council Official Records: 23rd Year, p. 7.

5. Security Council Official Records: 25th Year, p. 6, paragraph 21 (c).

6. Security Council Resolution 314 (1972), paragraph 6.

7. Fourth Report of the Sanctions Committee, June 16, 1971, United Nations Doc. S/10229.

8. Ibid., p. 13, paragraph 46.

9. Ibid., p. 14.

10. Ibid., p. 15.

11. The Rotenfels case reported in the Fifth Report of the Sanctions Committee, United Nations Doc. S/10852/Add. 1, Annex II, p. 19 ff.

12. The Sanctions Committee has published two Special Reports: Special Report of May 9, 1972, United Nations Doc. S/10632 and Second Special Report of April 15, 1973, United Nations Doc. S/10920.

13. See the Second Special Report of the Committee Established in Pursuance of Security Council Resolution 253 (1968) Concerning the Question of Southern Rhodesia (hereinafter referred to as Second Special Report), United Nations Doc. S/10920, April 15, 1973, p. 2.

14. This recommendation was contained in the First Special Report of the Committee (see United Nations Doc. S/10632, paragraph 19) and subsequently approved by the Security Council in Resolution 318 (1972).

15. Second Special Report, loc. cit., paragraph 10, 11.

16. Ibid., paragraph 12.

17. Ibid., paragraphs 14, 15.

18. One of the few reported instances of confiscation is Case No. 134 concerning a cargo of maize shipped from Beira to Alexandria on board the SS Bregaglia. Investigation by Egyptian authorities on information furnished by the United Kingdom led to the confiscation of the cargo. The Egyptian government donated the proceeds of the sale to the OAU Coordinating Committee for the liberation of Africa. See United Nations Doc. S/10852/Add. I, pp. 47-48, and the annex to the present study.

19. Second Special Report, loc. cit., paragraph 19.

20. Ibid., paragraph 23 (a).

21. Ibid., paragraph 23 (b) (i).

22. Ibid., paragraph 37.

23. Ibid., paragraph 23 (b) (iv).

24. Ibid., paragraph 26.

25. Ibid., paragraphs 24 (a), 25 (a), and 27.

26. Ibid., paragraph 40.

27. Ibid., paragraph 25 (c).
28. Ibid., paragraph 31.
29. Ibid., Part V.
30. Ibid., paragraphs 35, 36.
31. Ibid., paragraph 36.
32. Ibid., paragraphs 38, 39.
33. Security Council Resolution 333 (1973), May 22, 1973.
34. United Nations Security Council Doc. S/10928.

12

CONCLUSIONS

Having regard to the continuing nature of the United Nations involvement in Rhodesia, any conclusions that may be distilled from the present study must necessarily be somewhat tentative. Nevertheless, there would appear to be a sufficient accumulation of evidence with respect to certain aspects of the Rhodesian problem to justify a number of inductive observations. In so doing, it may be helpful to distinguish between sanctions as an instrument of international policy and sanctions as an institutional system.

As an instrument of international policy, sanctions have thus far patently failed in their primary objective of inducing political change in Rhodesia conformable to the demands of the international community. The failure of sanctions as a pragmatic device may be ascribed to various factors. In the first place, the sanctions policy has been incapacitated from its inception by the refusal of South Africa and Portugal to comply with the relevant Security Council Resolutions. The hemorrhage in the economic blockade resulting from South African and Portuguese noncompliance has been fatal to the policy as conceived. But even within the politically acceptable limits of the policy, sanctions have not been implemented with maximum effectiveness by a number of important states. In particular, several Western trading nations continued to engage in commercial relations with Rhodesia in breach of the letter or the spirit of Security Council sanctions long after the imposition of optional and partial sanctions in 1965 and 1966. Although the Sanctions Committee reports of suspected violations must be treated with the caution reserved for prima facie evidence, it is nevertheless suggestive and revealing, if not particularly surprising, that the governments whose authorities have most frequently been notified of suspected violations are West Germany, Holland, Japan, Greece, Switzerland, France, Italy, and Belgium. Indirectly, much of the responsibility for this state of affairs must fall on Britain. Although the United Kingdom authorities have compiled a scrupulous record on the enforcement of sanctions and have been by far the most prolific purveyor of information to the Sanctions Committee, it remains that British policy on Rhodesia has, on the whole, been too ambivalent to enable it to exert the quality of leadership in the United Nations that would compel respect from other nations. The Home-Smith Agreement of 1971, for example, was hardly the sort of exercise calculated to spur states to greater efforts in support of the economic blockade. The obvious desire of the British government to reach an agreement, any agreement, with the Smith regime has merely increased British vulnerability on the issue of enforcement, with the result that they failed even to publicly protest the singularly maladroit breach of sanctions by the United States pursuant to the passage of the Byrd amendment.

The open violation of sanctions by the United States is a severe blow to the prestige of the Security Council and the United Nations. Permanent members of the Security Council have special rights and obligations in the scheme of the Charter, and just as their veto power confers on them the right to block action of the Security Council, once a permanent member of the Security Council has acquiesced in such a decision either by an affirmative vote or an abstention, a subsequent failure to comply with that decision is a particularly grave breach of its obligations under the Charter and under general international law.

Two other debilitating factors, which have been explored in full in the preceding pages, are the lack of universality of United Nations membership, which led to the anomalous positions of Switzerland and West Germany, and the failure to apply the full range of mandatory sanctions immediately.

On another level, United Nations policy on Rhodesia has tended to overlook the important function of nongovernmental actors such as the multinational corporations and the trade unions. The difficulties encountered by governments and intergovernmental organizations alike in controlling the activities of multinational corporations are widely recognized, and the matter is now under review by more than one United Nations body. Given the size of the holdings and operations of several multinational corporations in southern Africa, the acquiescence in or rejection of the Rhodesian cause by them is bound to have enormous repercussions in Rhodesia. The role of a number of American corporations in securing the passage of the Byrd amendment, which has been well documented in the United Nations Association study referred to above, leaves little doubt as to where corporate power rests on this issue. What evidence is available, from time to time, suggests that the multinational corporations have not found it too difficult to pay lip service to the sanctions policy while at the same time ensuring the integrity of their investments in Rhodesia. But if management has not been particularly helpful, neither, it should be added, has labor. Trade unions can play a significant role in foreign policy as they have demonstrated on numerous occasions in the past. The refusal of United States longshoremen to unload vessels having engaged in trade with Cuba, or the more recent example of Australian and New Zealand longshoremen refusing to service French vessels in retaliation for the July 1973 French nuclear tests are examples of trade union foreign policy in action. The fragmentary mobilization of support by certain segments of the American labor movement against the Byrd amendment and the subsequent attempts to block shipments of Rhodesian chrome ore into the United States have, however, proved unsuccessful.

Despite all of the loopholes and difficulties, sanctions are nevertheless producing effects on the Rhodesian economy. There are persistent reports of a foreign exchange shortage and the running down of capital goods such as tractors and railway rolling stock. The import substitution industries, which have been largely responsible for enabling the Rhodesian economy to survive, are themselves threatened by a shortage of new machinery in the factories. The Rhodesian business community and the white population are beginning to feel the effects of sanctions, delayed though they may be.

If we examine sanctions as a system as distinct from an instrumentality, the Rhodesian experiment is undoubtedly one of the more interesting exercises in international organization functioning since 1945. It is important to bear in mind that the Rhodesian sanctions represent the first invocation of Chapter VII of the Charter, and they have been of considerable probative value in exploring the organization's capacity for enforcement of international obligations. One test of a system is its internal capacity for periodic evaluation and improvement. As evidenced by the Sanctions Committee's reports to the Security Council, the system in this case has proved surprisingly strong, having been in force now for upward of eight years, periodically reinforced and improved. Sanctions are now an accepted feature of the international landscape, and the use of sanctions as an instrument for attaining community goals in Rhodesia is no longer questioned. Indeed, as the most recent Security Council discussions demonstrate, there appears to be a wider acceptance of sanctions now than ever before. Furthermore, taken as example of international law making, the incorporation of international-level norms into domestic legal systems has been achieved without difficulty. From a systemic point of view, therefore, the real importance of sanctions is that they have shown the capacity within the United Nations for creating an instrument whereby the comportment of the individual member states can be measured in unusually concise and concrete terms. Thus, through the mechanism of the Sanctions Committee, it has been possible to determine the effects of noncompliance by South Africa and Portugal and to measure the compliance of more than 80 states. Thus, even though eight years of economic coercion and international ostracism would appear to have resulted in stalemate, the satisfaction among supporters of the Smith regime must, nevertheless, be tempered with the certain knowledge that the existing status quo is exceedingly precarious. As far as the United Nations is concerned, although sanctions have so far failed to achieve the organization's goals, they have nevertheless succeeded in denying legitimacy to the Rhodesian regime as well as imposing a heavy economic burden.

There can be no room for complacency, however, for in the years since UDI, the threat to the peace inherent in the Rhodesian situation has increased rather than diminished. Internal tension continues to grow, and there is evidence of a propensity toward externalization of the conflict, which would have the gravest consequences for the whole of southern Africa.

Internally, while the Smith regime has sought to consolidate its hold on the country entrenched behind an African-style system of apartheid, organized African opposition has continued despite the obstacles created by the state of emergency. In recent months, two significant political developments, which are indicative of both the potential for a peaceful settlement and a settlement by more violent means, have occurred. The first of these is the emergence of the African National Council (ANC) as a new African political force. Formed originally for the purpose of rejecting the 1971 settlement proposal, the ANC under the leadership of Bishop Abel Muzorewa has restored and revitalized the African political consciousness. But in sharp contrast to the moderate and nonviolent ANC are the Rhodesian liberation movements, the most important of which is the Front for the Liberation of Zimbabwe (Frolizi). Although guerilla activity in Rhodesia is still in a relatively embryonic stage—one recent estimate is that fewer than 150 guerrillas are operating in Rhodesia—and has been largely confined to the northeast in the pocket created by the Zambian and Mozambique borders, it has already created a siege mentality among Europeans. The Smith regime has responded to the guerrilla campaign with collective punishment of villages suspected of having harbored or assisted the guerrillas, the creation of a cordon sanitaire along the Mozambique border, and the execution of a number of captured guerrillas, none of which, in the light of historical experience, can be particularly reassuring for the white minority.

The externalization of the internal conflict poses a serious threat to the peace, which cannot be ignored even by those who cling to the belief that the Rhodesian situation is a domestic matter. The tension on the Zambian border (now closed) and persistent reports of the presence of South African paramilitary personnel in Rhodesia are only two manifestations of the potential for a wider conflict. More recently, detailed allegations of atrocities in Mozambique contained accounts of reprisal raids carried out by Rhodesian forces on the Mozambique territory in which men, women, and children were indiscriminately tortured and killed. These danger signals of incipient racial warfare cannot be ignored. The British Foreign Secretary, Sir Alec Douglas Home, has acknowledged that unless there is an evolutionary political settlement in Rhodesia, there could well be a confrontation not only in Rhodesia but on the rest of the Continent.

But what kind of evolutionary settlement and when? Is it to be a science fiction settlement along the lines of the Home-Smith terms of 1971 or a settlement providing for genuine African advancement within the five principles enunciated by the British government in 1964? The ANC is seeking immediate parity for African members of Parliament with Europeans, the immediate release of detainees and an amnesty for members of terrorist organizations, the repeal of the Land Tenure Act with the exception of the tribal trust lands provisions, the repeal of all discriminatory legislation, the establishment of an integrated school system, the appointment to ministries and the armed services on an equal racial quota basis, and a lower and broadening of the franchise qualifications for Africans. There is nothing in the comportment of the Smith regime to suggest that it is prepared to discuss any of these measures within the framework of a realistic timetable. In this connection it is interesting to note that Sir Roy Welensky, the veteran Rhodesian politician, believes that there will never be a more moderate African than Bishop Muzorewa of the ANC and that the longer a settlement is delayed, the greater is the risk of violent conflict.

In the final analysis, it is from this perspective that United Nations sanctions must be viewed for they would appear to constitute the only constructive alternative, as a strategy for securing a settlement conformable to the dictates of international public policy, between the endless procrastination upon the part of Whitehall and Salisbury and the evergrowing menace of armed conflict. In a Continent facing severe problems of economic development and political stability, a racial conflict in southern African would be nothing short of a catastrophe. It is therefore palpably in the interests of the international community to persevere with sanctions until justice in Rhodesia is achieved.

In April 1974 an event external to Rhodesia, which seems destined to alter the fragile equation upon which Rhodesian economic survival has depended, occurred. The overthrow of the Portuguese government of Marcello Caetano by elements of the army with the announced intention of seeking a cease-fire in the overseas territories and the devolution of these territories toward some form of independence or autonomy poses the most serious threat to the Smith regime since its unilateral declaration of independence (UDI). Throughout the gradual buildup of sanctions around Rhodesia, the Smith government was able to rely on the support of Portugal, safe in the knowledge that access to the Indian Ocean via Mozambique was assured. This reliance has now been shattered.

Rhodesia has depended upon the use of Mozambican ports for the bulk of its imports and exports. In 1972 Mozambique export trade with the principal market economy countries in Western Europe, Canada, Japan, Australia, and New Zealand reflected approximately $90 million of disguised Rhodesian exports. Should this avenue be closed, the Rhodesian economy will almost certainly contract even further, although it may be assumed that part of the trade may be diverted through South Africa. Just as serious and potentially even more dangerous than the economic consequences of a change of policy in Mozambique is the strategic impact. Guerilla activity emanating from Mozambique has been kept in check, thanks to the cooperation of Portuguese and Rhodesian forces. It seems clear that such cooperation in the future will diminish and eventually cease altogether. Deprived of Portuguese support, the Rhodesian forces will have a more difficult task in securing their eastern flank.

At the time of writing, it is difficult to predict the outcome of the new situation in Portugal and its repercussions in the overseas territories of Mozambique and Angola. It seems safe to say, however, that great changes are about to take place and that they are unlikely to be beneficial to Rhodesia. The Portuguese coup may prove to be the decisive element, the missing link, in the United Nations sanctions policy. If this is indeed the case, it will be one of the great ironies of history.

111

APPENDIXES

APPENDIX A: CHRONOLOGY OF UNITED NATIONS SECURITY COUNCIL RESOLUTIONS ON RHODESIA FROM 1965 TO 1973

Resolution 202 (1965)
of 6 May 1965

The Security Council,

Having examined the situation in Southern Rhodesia,

Recalling General Assembly resolutions 1514 (XV) of 14 December 1960, 1747 (XVI) of 28 June 1962, 1760 (XVII) of 31 October 1962, 1883 (XVIII) of 14 October 1963 and 1889 (XVIII) of 6 November 1963 and the resolutions of the Special Committee on the Situation with regard to the Implementation of the Declaration on the Granting of Independence to Colonial Countries and Peoples, especially its resolution of 22 April 1965,

Endorsing the requests which the General Assembly and the Special Committee have many times addressed to the United Kingdom of Great Britain and Northern Ireland to obtain:

(a) The release of all political prisoners, detainees and restrictees,

(b) The repeal of all repressive and discriminatory legislation, and in particular the Law and Order (Maintenance) Act and the Land Apportionment Act,

(c) The removal of all restrictions on political activity and the establishment of full democratic freedom and equality of political rights,

Noting that the Special Committee has drawn the attention of the Security Council to the grave situation prevailing in Southern Rhodesia and, in particular, to the serious implications of the elections announced to take place on 7 May 1965 under a constitution which has been rejected by the majority of the people of Southern Rhodesia and the abrogation of which has repeatedly been called for by the General Assembly and the Special Committee since 1962,

Deeply disturbed at the further worsening of the situation in the Territory due to the application of the aforementioned Constitution of 1961 and to recent events, especially the minority Government's threats of a unilateral declaration of independence,

1. Notes the United Kingdom Government's statement of 27 October 1964 specifying the conditions under which Southern Rhodesia might attain independence;

2. Notes further and approves the opinion of the majority of the population of Southern Rhodesia that the United Kingdom should convene a constitutional conference;

3. Requests the United Kingdom Government and all States Members of the United Nations not to accept a unilateral declaration of independence for Southern Rhodesia by the minority Government;

4. Requests the United Kingdom to take all necessary action to prevent a unilateral declaration of independence;

5. Requests the United Kingdom Government not to transfer under any circumstances to its colony of Southern Rhodesia, as at present governed, any of the powers of attributes of sovereignty, but to promote the country's attainment of independence by a democratic system of government in accordance with the aspirations of the majority of the population;

6. Further requests the United Kingdom Government to enter into consultations with all concerned with a view to convening a conference of all political parties in order to adopt new constitutional provisions acceptable to the majority of the people of Southern Rhodesia, so that the earliest possible date may be set for independence;

7. Decides to keep the question of Southern Rhodesia on its agenda.

> Adopted at the 1202nd meeting by 7 votes to none, with 4 abstentions (France, Union of Soviet Socialist Republics, United Kingdom of Great Britain and Northern Ireland, United States of America).

Resolution 216 (1965)
of 12 November 1965

The Security Council
1. Decides to condemn the unilateral declaration of independence made by a racist minority in Southern Rhodesia;

2. Decides to call upon all States not to recognize this illegal racist minority regime in Southern Rhodesia and to refrain from rendering any assistance to this illegal regime.

> Adopted at the 1258th meeting by 10 votes to none, with 1 abstention (France).

Resolution 217 (1965)
of 20 November 1965

The Security Council,
Deeply concerned about the situation in Southern Rhodesia,

Considering that the illegal authorities in Southern Rhodesia have proclaimed independence and that the Government of the United Kingdom of Great Britain and Northern Ireland, as the administering Power, looks upon this as an act of rebellion,

Noting that the Government of the United Kingdom has taken certain measures to meet the situation and that to be effective these measures should correspond to the gravity of the situation,

1. Determines that the situation resulting from the proclamation of independence by the illegal authorities in Southern Rhodesia is extremely grave, that the Government of the United Kingdom of Great Britain and Northern Ireland should put an end to it and that its continuance in time constitutes a threat to international peace and security;

2. Reaffirms its resolution 216 (1965) of 12 November 1965 and General Assembly resolution 1514 (XV) of 14 December 1960;

3. Condemns the usurpation of power by a racist settler minority in Southern Rhodesia and regards the declaration of independence by it as having no legal validity;

4. Calls upon the Government of the United Kingdom to quell this rebellion of the racist minority;

5. Further calls upon the Government of the United Kingdom to take all other appropriate measures which would prove effective in eliminating the authority of the usurpers and in bringing the minority regime in Southern Rhodesia to an immediate end;

6. Calls upon all States not to recognize this illegal authority and not to entertain any diplomatic or other relations with it;

7. Calls upon the Government of the United Kingdom, as the working of the Constitution of 1961 has broken down, to take immediate measures in order to allow the people of Southern Rhodesia to determine their own future consistent with the objectives of General Assembly resolution 1514 (XV);

8. Calls upon all States to refrain from any action which would assist and encourage the illegal regime and, in particular, to desist from providing it with arms, equipment and military material, and to do their utmost in order to break all economic relations with Southern Rhodesia, including an embargo on oil and petroleum products;

9. Calls upon the Government of the United Kingdom to enforce urgently and with vigor all the measures it has announced, as well as those mentioned in paragraph 8 above;

10. Calls upon the Organization of African Unity to do all in its power to assist in the implementation of the present resolution, in conformity with Chapter VIII of the Charter of the United Nations;

11. Decides to keep the question under review in order to examine what other measures it may deem it necessary to take.

Adopted at the 1265th meeting by 10 votes to none, with 1 abstention (France).

Resolution 221 (1966)
of 9 April 1966

The Security Council,

Recalling its resolutions 216 (1965) of 12 November 1965 and
217 (1965) of 20 November 1965 and in particular its call to all States
to do their utmost to break off economic relations with Southern
Rhodesia, including an embargo on oil and petroleum products,

Gravely concerned at reports that substantial supplies of oil
may reach Southern Rhodesia as the result of an oil tanker having
arrived at Beira and the approach of a further tanker which may lead
to the resumption of pumping through the Companhia do Pipeline
Moçambique Rodésias pipeline with the acquiescence of the Portuguese
authorities,

Considering that such supplies will afford great assistance and
encouragement to the illegal regime in Southern Rhodesia, thereby
enabling it to remain longer in being,

1. Determines that the resulting situation constitutes a threat
to the peace;

2. Calls upon the Portuguese Government not to permit oil to
be pumped through the pipeline from Beira to Southern Rhodesia;

3. Calls upon the Portuguese Government not to receive at
Beira oil destined for Southern Rhodesia;

4. Calls upon all States to ensure the diversion of any of their
vessels reasonably believed to be carrying oil destined for Southern
Rhodesia which may be en route for Beira;

5. Calls upon the Government of the United Kingdom of Great
Britain and Northern Ireland to prevent, by the use of force if necessary, the arrival at Beira of vessels reasonably believed to be carrying oil destined for Southern Rhodesia, and empowers the United
Kingdom to arrest and detain the tanker known as the Joanna V upon
her departure from Beira in the event her oil cargo is discharged
there.

> Adopted at the 1277th meeting by 10 votes to none,
> with 5 abstentions (Bulgaria, France, Mali, Union
> of Soviet Socialist Republics, Uruguay).

Resolution 232 (1966)
of 16 December 1966

The Security Council,

Reaffirming its resolutions 216 (1965) of 12 November 1965,
217 (1965) of 20 November 1965 and 221 (1966) of 9 April 1966, and
in particular its appeal to all States to do their utmost to break off
economic relations with Southern Rhodesia,

Deeply concerned that the Council's efforts so far and the measures taken by the administering Power have failed to bring the rebellion in Southern Rhodesia to an end,

Reaffirming that, to the extent not superseded in the present resolution, the measures provided for in resolution 217 (1965), as well as those initiated by Member States in implementation of that resolution, shall continue in effect,

Acting in accordance with Articles 39 and 41 of the United Nations Charter,

1. Determines that the present situation in Southern Rhodesia constitutes a threat to international peace and security;

2. Decides that all States Members of the United Nations shall prevent:

(a) The import into their territories of asbestos, iron ore, chrome, pig-iron, sugar, tobacco, copper, meat and meat products and hides, skins and leather originating in Southern Rhodesia and exported therefrom after the date of the present resolution;

(b) Any activities by their nationals or in their territories which promote or are calculated to promote the export of these commodities from Southern Rhodesia and any dealings by their nationals or in their territories in any of these commodities originating in Southern Rhodesia and exported therefrom after the date of the present resolution, including in particular any transfer of funds to Southern Rhodesia for the purposes of such activities or dealings;

(c) Shipment in vessels or aircraft of their registration of any of these commodities originating in Southern Rhodesia and exported therefrom after the date of the present resolution;

(d) Any activities by their nationals or in their territories which promote or are calculated to promote the sale or shipment to Southern Rhodesia of arms, ammunition of all types, military aircraft, military vehicles, and equipment and materials for the manufacture and maintenance of arms and ammunition in Southern Rhodesia;

(e) Any activities by their nationals or in their territories which promote or are calculated to promote the supply to Southern Rhodesia of all other aircraft and motor vehicles and of equipment and materials for the manufacture, assembly, or maintenance of aircraft and motor vehicles in Southern Rhodesia; the shipment in vessels and aircraft of their registration of any such goods destined for Southern Rhodesia; and any activities by their nationals or in their territories which promote or are calculated to promote the manufacture or assembly of aircraft or motor vehicles in Southern Rhodesia;

(f) Participation in their territories or territories under their administration or in land or air transport facilities or by their nationals or vessels of their registration in the supply of oil or oil products to Southern Rhodesia; notwithstanding any contracts entered into or licenses granted before the date of the present resolution;

3. Reminds Member States that the failure or refusal by any of them to implement the present resolution shall constitute a violation of Article 25 of the United Nations Charter;

4. Reaffirms the inalienable rights of the people of Southern Rhodesia to freedom and independence in accordance with the Declaration on the Granting of Independence to Colonial Countries and Peoples contained in General Assembly resolution 1514 (XV) of 14 December 1960, and recognizes the legitimacy of their struggle to secure the enjoyment of their rights as set forth in the Charter of the United Nations;

5. Calls upon all States not to render financial or other economic aid to the illegal racist regime in Southern Rhodesia;

6. Calls upon all States Members of the United Nations to carry out this decision of the Security Council in accordance with Article 25 of the United Nations Charter;

7. Urges, having regard to the principles stated in Article 2 of the United Nations Charter, States not Members of the United Nations to act in accordance with the provisions of paragraph 2 of the present resolution;

8. Calls upon States Members of the United Nations or members of the specialized agencies to report to the Secretary-General the measures which each has taken in accordance with the provisions of paragraph 2 of the present resolution;

9. Requests the Secretary-General to report to the Council on the progress of the implementation of the present resolution, the first report to be submitted not later than 1 March 1967;

10. Decides to keep this item on its agenda for further action as appropriate in the light of developments.

> Adopted at the 1340th meeting by 11 votes to none, with 4 abstentions (Bulgaria, France, Mali, Union of Soviet Socialist Republics).

Resolution 253 (1968)
of 29 May 1968

The Security Council,

Recalling and reaffirming its resolutions 216 (1965) of 12 November 1965, 217 (1965) of 20 November 1965, 221 (1966) of 9 April 1966, and 232 (1966) of 16 December 1966,

Taking note of resolution 2262 (XXII) adopted by the General Assembly on 3 November 1967,

Noting with great concern that the measures taken so far have failed to bring the rebellion in Southern Rhodesia to an end,

Reaffirming that, to the extent not superseded in this resolution, the measures provided for in resolutions 217 (1965) of 20 November 1965 and 232 (1966) of 16 December 1966, as well as those initiated by Member States in implementation of those resolutions, shall continue in effect,

Gravely concerned that the measures taken by the Security Council have not been complied with by all States and that some States, contrary to resolution 232 (1966) of the Security Council and to their obligations under Article 25 of the Charter of the United Nations, have failed to prevent trade with the illegal regime in Southern Rhodesia,

Condemning the recent inhuman executions carried out by the illegal regime in Southern Rhodesia which have flagrantly affronted the conscience of mankind and have been universally condemned,

Affirming the primary responsibility of the Government of the United Kingdom to enable the people of Southern Rhodesia to achieve self-determination and independence, and in particular their responsibility for dealing with the prevailing situation,

Recognizing the legitimacy of the struggle of the people of Southern Rhodesia to secure the enjoyment of their rights as set forth in the Charter of the United Nations and in conformity with the objectives of General Assembly resolution 1514 (XV) of 14 December 1960,

Reaffirming its determination that the present situation in Southern Rhodesia constitutes a threat to international peace and security,

Acting under Chapter VII of the Charter of the United Nations,

1. Condemns all measures of political repression, including arrests, detentions, trials and executions which violate fundamental freedoms and rights of the people of Southern Rhodesia, and calls upon the Government of the United Kingdom to take all possible measures to put an end to such actions;

2. Calls upon the United Kingdom as the administering Power in the discharge of its responsibility to take urgently all effective measures to bring to an end the rebellion in Southern Rhodesia, and enable the people to secure the enjoyment of their rights as set forth in the Charter of the United Nations and in conformity with the objectives of General Assembly resolution 1514 (XV);

3. Decides that, in furtherance of the objective of ending the rebellion, all States Members of the United Nations shall prevent:

(a) The import into their territories of all commodities and products originating in Southern Rhodesia and exported therefrom after the date of this resolution (whether or not the commodities or products are for consumption or processing in their territories, whether or not they are imported in bond and whether or not any special legal status with respect to the import of goods is enjoyed by the port or other place where they are imported or stored);

(b) Any activities by their nationals or in their territories which would promote or are calculated to promote the export of any commodities or products from Southern Rhodesia; and any dealings by their nationals or in their territories in any commodities or products originating in Southern Rhodesia and exported therefrom after the date of this resolution, including in particular any transfer of funds to Southern Rhodesia for the purposes of such activities or dealings;

(c) The shipment in vessels or aircraft of their registration or under charter to their nationals, or the carriage (whether or not in bond) by land transport facilities across their territories of any commodities or products originating in Southern Rhodesia and exported therefrom after the date of this resolution;

(d) The sale or supply by their nationals or from their territories of any commodities or products (whether or not originating in their territories, but not including supplies intended strictly for medical purposes, educational equipment and material for use in schools and other educational institutions, publications, news material and, in special humanitarian circumstances, food-stuffs) to any person or body in Southern Rhodesia or to any other person or body for the purposes of any business carried on in or operated from Southern Rhodesia, and any activities by their nationals or in their territories which promote or are calculated to promote such sale or supply;

(e) The shipment in vessels or aircraft of their registration, or under charter to their nationals, or the carriage (whether or not in bond) by land transport facilities across their territories of any such commodities or products which are consigned to any person or body in Southern Rhodesia, or to any other person or body for the purposes of any business carried on in or operated from Southern Rhodesia;

4. Decides that all States Members of the United Nations shall not make available to the illegal regime in Southern Rhodesia or to any commercial, industrial or public utility undertaking, including tourist enterprises, in Southern Rhodesia any funds for investment or any other financial or economic resources and shall prevent their nationals and any persons within their territories from making available to the regime or to any such undertaking any such funds or resources and from remitting any other funds to persons or bodies within Southern Rhodesia, except payments exclusively for pensions or for strictly medical, humanitarian or educational purposes or for the provision of news material and in special humanitarian circumstances, foodstuffs;

5. Decides that all States Members of the United Nations shall:

(a) Prevent the entry into their territories, save on exceptional humanitarian grounds, of any person travelling on a Southern Rhodesian passport, regardless of its date of issue, or on a purported passport issued by or on behalf of the illegal regime in Southern Rhodesia;

(b) Take all possible measures to prevent the entry into their territories of persons whom they have resaon to believe to be ordinarily resident in Southern Rhodesia and whom they have reason to believe to have furthered or encouraged, or to be likely to further or encourage, the unlawful actions of the illegal regime in Southern Rhodesia or any activities which are calculated to evade any measure decided upon in this resolution or resolution 232 (1966) of 16 December 1966;

6. Decides that all States Members of the United Nations shall prevent airline companies constituted in their territories and aircraft of their registration or under charter to their nationals from operating to or from Southern Rhodesia and from linking up with any airline company constituted or aircraft registered in Southern Rhodesia;

7. Decides that all States Members of the United Nations shall give effect to the decisions set out in operative paragraphs 3, 4, 5 and 6 of this resolution notwithstanding any contract entered into or licence granted before the date of this resolution;

8. Calls upon all States Members of the United Nations or of the specialized agencies to take all possible measures to prevent activities by their nationals and persons in their territories promoting, assisting or encouraging emigration to Southern Rhodesia, with a view to stopping such emigration;

9. Requests all States Members of the United Nations or of the specialized agencies to take all possible further action under Article 41 of the Charter to deal with the situation in Southern Rhodesia, not excluding any of the measures provided in that Article;

10. Emphasizes the need for the withdrawal of all consular and trade representation in Southern Rhodesia, in addition to the provisions of operative paragraph 6 of resolution 217 (1965);

11. Calls upon all States Members of the United Nations to carry out these decisions of the Security Council in accordance with Article 25 of the Charter of the United Nations and reminds them that failure or refusal by any one of them to do so would constitute a violation of that Article;

12. Deplores the attitude of States that have not complied with their obligations under Article 25 of the Charter, and censures in particular those States which have persisted in trading with the illegal regime in defiance of the resolutions of the Security Council, and which have given active assistance to the regime;

13. Urges all States Members of the United Nations to render moral and material assistance to the people of Southern Rhodesia in their struggle to achieve their freedom and independence;

14. Urges, having regard to the principles stated in Article 2 of the Charter of the United Nations, States not Members of the United Nations to act in accordance with the provisions of the present resolution;

15. Requests States Members of the United Nations, the United Nations Organization, the specialized agencies, and other international organizations in the United Nations system to extend assistance to Zambia as a matter of priority with a view to helping it solve such special economic problems as it may be confronted with arising from the carrying out of these decisions of the Security Council;

16. Calls upon all States Members of the United Nations, and in particular those with primary responsibility under the Charter for the maintenance of international peace and security, to assist effectively in the implementation of the measures called for by the present resolution;

17. Considers that the United Kingdom as the administering Power should ensure that no settlement is reached without taking into account the views of the people of Southern Rhodesia, and in particular the political parties favoring majority rule, and that it is acceptable to the people of Southern Rhodesia as a whole;

18. Calls upon all States Members of the United Nations or of the specialized agencies to report to the Secretary-General by 1 August 1968 on measures taken to implement the present resolution;

19. Requests the Secretary-General to report to the Security Council on the progress of the implementation of this resolution, the first report to be made not later than 1 September 1968;

20. Decides to establish, in accordance with rule 28 of the provisional rules of procedure of the Security Council, a committee of the Security Council to undertake the following tasks and to report to it with its observations:

(a) To examine such reports on the implementation of the present resolution as are submitted by the Secretary-General;

(b) To seek from any States Members of the United Nations or of the specialized agencies such further information regarding the trade of that State (including information regarding the commodities and products exempted from the prohibition contained in operative paragraph 3 (d) above) or regarding any activities by any nationals of that State or in its territories that may constitute an evasion of the measure decided upon in this resolution as it may consider necessary for the proper discharge of its duty to report to the Security Council;

21. Requests the United Kingdom, as the administering Power, to give maximum assistance to the committee, and to provide the committee with any information which it may receive in order that the measures envisaged in this resolution and resolution 232 (1966) may be rendered fully effective;

22. Calls upon all States Members of the United Nations, or of the specialized agencies, as well as the specialized agencies themselves, to supply such further information as may be sought by the Committee in pursuance of this resolution;

23. Decides to maintain this item on its agenda for further action as appropriate in the light of developments.

Adopted unanimously at the 1428th meeting.

Resolution 277 (1970)
of 18 March 1970

The Security Council,

Reaffirming its resolutions 216 (1965) of 12 November 1965, 217 (1965) of 20 November 1965, 221 (1966) of 9 April 1966, 232 (1966) of 16 December 1966 and 253 (1968) of 29 May 1968,

Reaffirming that, to the extent not superseded in the present resolution, the measures provided for in resolutions 217 (1965), 232 (1966) and 253 (1968), as well as those initiated by Member States in implementation of those resolutions, shall continue in effect,

Taking into account the reports of the Committee established in pursuance of Security Council resolution 253 (1968),

Noting with grave concern that:

(a) The measures so far taken have failed to bring the rebellion in Southern Rhodesia to an end,

(b) Some States, contrary to resolutions 232 (1966) and 253 (1968) of the Security Council and to their obligations under Article 25 of the Charter of the United Nations, have failed to prevent trade with the illegal regime of Southern Rhodesia,

(c) The Governments of the Republic of South Africa and Portugal have continued to give assistance to the illegal regime of Southern Rhodesia, thus diminishing the effects of the measures decided upon by the Security Council,

(d) The situation in Southern Rhodesia continues to deteriorate as a result of the introduction by the illegal regime of new measures, including the purported assumption of republican status, aimed at repressing the African people in violation of General Assembly resolution 1514 (XV) of 14 December 1960,

Recognizing the legitimacy of the struggle of the people of Southern Rhodesia to secure the enjoyment of their rights as set forth in the Charter and in conformity with the objectives of General Assembly resolution 1514 (XV),

Reaffirming that the present situation in Southern Rhodesia constitutes a threat to international peace and security,

Acting under Chapter VII of the Charter,

1. Condemns the illegal proclamation of republican status of the Territory by the illegal regime in Southern Rhodesia;

2. Decides that Member States shall refrain from recognizing this illegal regime or from rendering any assistance to it;

3. Calls upon Member States to take appropriate measures, at the national level, to ensure that any act performed by officials and institutions of the illegal regime in Southern Rhodesia shall not be accorded any recognition, official or otherwise, including judicial notice, by the competent organs of their State;

4. Reaffirms the primary responsibility of the Government of the United Kingdom of Great Britain and Northern Ireland to enable the people of Zimbabwe to exercise their right to self-determination and independence, in accordance with the Charter of the United Nations and in conformity with General Assembly resolution 1514 (XV), and urges that Government to discharge fully its responsibility;

5. Condemns all measures of political repression, including arrests, detentions, trials and executions, which violate fundamental freedoms and rights of the people of Southern Rhodesia;

6. Condemns the policies of the Governments of South Africa and Portugal, which continue to maintain political, economic, military, and other relations with the illegal regime in Southern Rhodesia in violation of the relevant resolutions of the United Nations;

7. Demands the immediate withdrawal of South African police and armed personnel from the Territory of Southern Rhodesia;

8. Calls upon Member States to take more stringent measures in order to prevent any circumvention by their nationals, organizations, companies and other institutions of their nationality, of the decisions taken by the Security Council in resolutions 232 (1966) and 253 (1968), all provisions of which shall fully remain in force;

9. Decides, in accordance with Article 41 of the Charter and in furthering the objective of ending the rebellion, that Member States shall:

(a) Immediately sever all diplomatic, consular, trade, military and other relations that they may have with the illegal regime in Southern Rhodesia, and terminate any representation that they may maintain in the Territory;

(b) Immediately interrupt any existing means of transportation to and from Southern Rhodesia;

10. Requests the Government of the United Kingdom, as the administering Power, to rescind or withdraw any existing agreements on the basis of which foreign consular, trade and other representation may at present be maintained in or with Southern Rhodesia;

11. Requests Member States to take all possible further action under Article 41 of the Charter to deal with the situation in Southern Rhodesia, not excluding any of the measures provided in that Article;

12. Calls upon Member States to take appropriate action to suspend any membership or associate membership that the illegal regime of Southern Rhodesia has in the specialized agencies of the United Nations;

13. Urges member States of any international or regional organizations to suspend the membership of the illegal regime of Southern Rhodesia from their respective organizations and to refuse any request for membership from that regime;

14. Urges Member States to increase moral and material assistance to the people of Southern Rhodesia in their legitimate struggle to achieve freedom and independence;

15. Requests the specialized agencies and other international organizations concerned, in consultation with the Organization of African Unity, to give aid and assistance to refugees from Southern Rhodesia and those who are suffering from oppression by the illegal regime of Southern Rhodesia;

16. Requests Member States, the United Nations, the specialized agencies and other international organizations in the United Nations system to make an urgent effort to increase their assistance to Zambia as a matter of priority with a view to helping it solve such special economic problems as it may be confronted with arising from the carrying out of the decisions of the Security Council on this question;

17. Calls upon Member States, in particular those with primary responsibility under the Charter for the maintenance of international peace and security, to assist effectively in the implementation of the measures called for by the present resolution;

18. Urges, having regard to the principle stated in Article 2 of the Charter, States not Members of the United Nations to act in accordance with the provisions of the present resolution;

19. Calls upon Member States to report to the Secretary-General by 1 June 1970 on the measures taken to implement the present resolution;

20. Requests the Secretary-General to report to the Security Council on the progress of the implementation of the present resolution, the first report to be submitted no later than 1 July 1970;

21. Decides that the Committee of the Security Council established in pursuance of resolution 253 (1968), in accordance with rule 28 of the provisional rules of procedure of the Council, shall be entrusted with the responsibility of:

(a) Examining such reports on the implementation of the present resolution as will be submitted by the Secretary-General;

(b) Seeking from Member States such further information regarding the effective implementation of the provisions laid down in the present resolution as it may consider necessary for the proper discharge of its duty to report to the Security Council;

(c) Studying ways and means by which Member States could carry out more effectively the decisions of the Security Council regarding sanctions against the illegal regime of Southern Rhodesia and making recommendations to the Council;

22. Requests the United Kingdom, as the administering Power, to continue to give maximum assistance to the Committee and to provide the Committee with any information it may receive in order that the measures envisaged in the present resolution as well as resolutions 232 (1966) and 253 (1968) may be rendered fully effective;

23. Calls upon Member States, as well as the specialized agencies, to supply such information as may be sought by the Committee in pursuance of the present resolution;

24. Decides to maintain this item on its agenda for further action as appropriate in the light of developments.

Adopted at the 1535th meeting by 14 votes to none, with one abstention (Spain).

Resolution 288 (1970)
of 17 November 1970

The Security Council,

Having considered the question of Southern Rhodesia,

Reaffirming its resolutions 216 (1965) of 12 November 1965, 217 (1965) of 20 November 1965, 221 (1966) of 9 April 1966, 232 (1966) of 16 December 1966, 253 (1968) of 29 May 1968 and 277 (1970) of 18 March 1970,

Gravely concerned that certain States have not complied with the provisions of resolutions 232 (1966), 253 (1968) and 277 (1970), contrary to their obligations under Article 25 of the Charter of the United Nations,

Reaffirming the primary responsibility of the Government of the United Kingdom of Great Britain and Northern Ireland to enable the people of Southern Rhodesia to achieve self-determination and independence, and in particular their responsibility of bringing the illegal declaration of independence to an end,

Taking into account the third report of the Committee established in pursuance of Security Council resolution 253 (1968),

Acting in accordance with previous decisions of the Security Council on Southern Rhodesia, taken under Chapter VII of the Charter,

1. Reaffirms its condemnation of the illegal declaration of independence in Southern Rhodesia;

2. Calls upon the United Kingdom of Great Britain and Northern Ireland, as the administering Power in the discharge of its responsibility, to take urgent and effective measures to bring to an end the

illegal rebellion in Southern Rhodesia and enable the people to exercise their right to self-determination, in accordance with the Charter of the United Nations and in conformity with the objectives of General Assembly resolution 1514 (XV) of 14 December 1960;

3. Decides that the present sanctions against Southern Rhodesia shall remain in force;

4. Urges all States to fully implement all Security Council resolutions pertaining to Southern Rhodesia, in accordance with their obligations under Article 25 of the Charter, and deplores the attitude of those States which have persisted in giving moral, political and economic assistance to the illegal regime;

5. Further urges all States, in furtherance of the objectives of the Security Council, not to grant any form of recognition to the illegal regime in Southern Rhodesia;

6. Decides to remain actively seized of the matter.

Adopted unanimously at the 1557th meeting.

Resolution 314 (1972)
of 28 February 1972

The Security Council,

Having considered the recent developments concerning the question of Southern Rhodesia,

Recalling its resolutions 216 (1965) of 12 November 1965, 217 (1965), of 20 November 1965, 221 (1966) of 9 April 1966, 232 (1966) of 16 December 1966, 253 (1968) of 29 May 1968, 277 (1970) of 18 March 1970 and 288 (1970) of 17 November 1970,

Gravely concerned that certain States have not complied with the provisions of resolution 253 (1968), contrary to their obligations under Article 25 of the Charter of the United Nations,

Taking into account the fourth report of the Committee established in pursuance of Security Council resolution 253 (1968) and its interim report of 3 December 1971,

Acting in accordance with previous decisions of the Security Council on Southern Rhodesia, taken under Chapter VII of the Charter,

1. Reaffirms its decision that the present sanctions against Southern Rhodesia shall remain fully in force until the aims and objectives set out in resolution 253 (1968) are completely achieved;

2. Urges all States to implement fully all Security Council resolutions establishing sanctions against Southern Rhodesia, in accordance with their obligations under Article 25 and Article 2, paragraph 6, of the Charter of the United Nations and deplores the attitude of those States which have persisted in giving moral, political and economic assistance to the illegal regime;

3. Declares that any legislation passed, or act taken, by any State with a view to permitting, directly or indirectly, the importation from Southern Rhodesia of any commodity falling within the scope of the obligations imposed by resolution 253 (1968), including chrome ore, would undermine sanctions and would be contrary to the obligations of States;

4. Calls upon all States to refrain from taking any measures that would in any way permit or facilitate the importation from Southern Rhodesia of commodities falling within the scope of the obligations imposed by resolution 253 (1968), including chrome ore;

5. Draws the attention of all States to the need for increasing vigilance in implementing the provisions of resolution 253 (1968) and, accordingly, calls upon them to take more effective measures to ensure full implementation of the sanctions;

6. Requests the Committee established in pursuance of Security Council resolution 253 (1968) to meet, as a matter of urgency, to consider ways and means by which the implementation of sanctions may be ensured and to submit to the Council, not later than 15 April 1972, a report contained recommendations in this respect, including any suggestions that the Committee might wish to make concerning its terms of reference and any other measures designed to ensure the effectiveness of its work;

7. Requests the Secretary-General to provide all appropriate assistance to the Committee in the discharge of its task.

> Adopted at the 1645th meeting by 13 votes to none, with 2 abstentions (United Kingdom of Great Britain and Northern Ireland, United States of America).

Resolution 318 (1972)
of 28 July 1972

The Security Council,

Recalling its resolution 314 (1972) of 28 February 1972, in which it requested the Committee established in pursuance of Security Council resolution 253 (1968) of 29 May 1968 to consider ways and means by which the implementation of sanctions might be ensured and to submit a report containing recommendations in this respect, including any suggestions that the Committee might wish to make concerning its terms of reference and any other measures designed to ensure the effectiveness of its work,

Having considered the special report of the Committee established in pursuance of Security Council resolution 253 (1968),

Mindful of the need to strengthen the machinery established by the Security Council in order to ensure proper implementation of the relevant resolutions of the Council,

Recalling further that, as stated in previous resolutions of the Security Council, the present sanctions against Southern Rhodesia shall remain fully in force until the aims and objectives set out in resolution 253 (1968) are completely achieved,

Gravely concerned that certain States have not complied with the provisions of resolution 253 (1968), contrary to their obligations under Article 25 of the Charter of the United Nations,

1. Reaffirms the inalienable right of the people of Southern Rhodesia to self-determination and independence;

2. Recognizes the legitimacy of the struggle of the people of Southern Rhodesia to secure the enjoyment of their rights, as set forth in the Charter of the United Nations and in conformity with the objectives of General Assembly resolution 1514 (XV) of 14 December 1960;

3. Takes note with appreciation of the special report of the Committee established in pursuance of Security Council resolution 253 (1968);

4. Approves the recommendations and suggestions contained in section III of the special report;

5. Calls upon all States continuing to have economic and other relations with Southern Rhodesia to end such relations immediately;

6. Demands that all Member States scrupulously carry out their obligations to implement fully Security Council resolutions 253 (1968), 277 (1970) of 18 March 1970 and 314 (1972);

7. Condemns all acts violating the provisions of Security Council resolutions 253 (1968), 277 (1970) and 314 (1972);

8. Calls upon all States to co-operate fully with the Security Council in the effective implementation of sanctions and to give the Council all the necessary assistance that may be required of them towards the fulfilment of this task;

9. Again draws the attention of all States to the need for increasing vigilance in all matters relating to sanctions and, accordingly, urges them to review the adequacy of the legislation and the practices followed so far and, if necessary, to take more effective measures to ensure full implementation of all provisions of Security Council resolutions 253 (1968), 277 (1970) and 314 (1972);

10. Requests the Secretary-General to provide all appropriate assistance to the Security Council Committee established in pursuance of resolution 253 (1968) concerning the question of Southern Rhodesia in the discharge of its responsibilities.

Adopted at the 1655th meeting by 14 votes to none, with 1 abstention (United States of America).

Resolution 320 (1972)
of 29 September 1972

The Security Council,

Recalling its resolution 253 (1968) of 29 May 1968 and subsequent resolutions in which all States are required to implement and make effective the economic, political and other sanctions against Southern Rhodesia (Zimbabwe) decided upon by the Council in furtherance of the objective of ending the rebellion in that territory,

Taking into account its resolutions 314 (1972) of 28 February 1972 and 318 (1972) of 28 July 1972 concerning the co-operation and obligations of States and the measures necessary to ensure the scrupulous observance and strict implementation of sanctions,

Deeply concerned that, despite their obligations under Article 25 of the Charter of the United Nations, several States continue to violate sanctions covertly and overtly in contravention of the provisions of resolution 253 (1968),

Gravely concerned about the detrimental consequences which violations could cause to the effectiveness of sanctions and, in the wider sense, to the authority of the Council,

Deeply concerned by the report of the United States of America that it has authorized the importation of chrome ore and other minerals from Southern Rhodesia (Zimbabwe),

Condemning the refusal of South Africa and Portugal to co-operate with the United Nations in the observance and implementation of sanctions against Southern Rhodesia (Zimbabwe),

1. Reaffirms its decision that sanctions against Southern Rhodesia (Zimbabwe) shall remain fully in force until the aims and objectives set out in resolution 253 (1968) are completely achieved;

2. Calls upon all States to implement fully all Security Council resolutions establishing sanctions against Southern Rhodesia (Zimbabwe), in accordance with Article 25 and Article 2, paragraph 6, of the Charter of the United Nations;

3. Urges the United States of America to co-operate fully with the United Nations in the effective implementation of sanctions;

4. Requests the Security Council Committee established in pursuance of resolution 253 (1968) concerning the question of Southern Rhodesia to undertake, as a matter of urgency, consideration of the type of action which could be taken in view of the open and persistent refusal of South Africa and Portugal to implement sanctions against the illegal regime in Southern Rhodesia (Zimbabwe) and to report to the Council not later than 31 January 1973;

5. Further requests the Committee to examine and submit a report to the Security Council not later than 31 January 1973 on all proposals and suggestions made at the 1663rd to 1666th meetings of

the Council for extending the scope and improving the effectiveness
of sanctions against Southern Rhodesia (Zimbabwe).

> Adopted at the 1666th meeting by 13 votes to none,
> with 2 abstentions (United Kingdom of Great Britain
> and Northern Ireland, United States of America).

Resolution 328 (1973)
Adopted by the Security Council at its 1694th meeting,
on 10 March 1973

The Security Council,

Having considered with appreciation the report of the Security
Council Special Mission established under resolution 326 (1973) of 2
February 1973,

Having heard further a statement by the Permanent Representative of the Republic of Zambia,

Recalling its resolutions 277 (1970) and 326 (1973),

Reaffirming that the situation in Southern Rhodesia constitutes
a threat to international peace and security,

Gravely concerned at the persistent refusal of the regime of
South Africa to respond to the demands contained in its resolutions
277 (1970) and 326 (1973) for the immediate withdrawal of its military
and armed forces from Southern Rhodesia and convinced that this
constitutes a serious challenge to the authority of the Security Council,

Bearing in mind that the Government of the United Kingdom,
as the administering Power, has the primary responsibility for putting
an end to the illegal racist minority regime and for transferring
effective power to the people of Zimbabwe on the basis of the principle
of majority rule,

Reaffirming the inalienable right of the people of Zimbabwe
to self-determination and independence in accordance with General
Assembly resolution 1514 (XV) and the legitimacy of their struggle
to secure the enjoyment of their right as set forth in the Charter of
the United Nations,

1. Endorses the assessment and conclusions of the Special
Mission established under resolution 326 (1973);

2. Affirms that the state of tension has been heightened
following the recent provocative and aggressive acts committed by
the illegal regime of Southern Rhodesia against the Republic of
Zambia;

3. Declares that the only effective solution to this grave
situation lies in the exercise by the people of Zimbabwe of their
right to self-determination and independence in accordance with
General Assembly resolution 1514 (XV);

4. Strongly condemns the racist regime of South Africa for its persistent refusal to withdraw its military and armed forces from Southern Rhodesia;

5. Reiterates its demand for the immediate withdrawal of South African military and armed forces from Southern Rhodesia and from the border of that territory with Zambia;

6. Urges the Security Council Committee established in pursuance of resolution 253 (1968) concerning the question of Southern Rhodesia to expedite the preparation of its report undertaken under Security Council resolution 320 (1972), taking into account all proposals and suggestions for extending the scope and improving the effectiveness of sanctions against Southern Rhodesia (Zimbabwe);

7. Requests all Governments to take stringent measures to enforce and ensure full compliance by all individuals and organizations under their jurisdiction with the sanctions policy against Southern Rhodesia and calls upon all Governments to continue to treat the racist minority regime in Southern Rhodesia as wholly illegal;

8. Urges the United Kingdom as the administering Power to convene as soon as possible a national Constitutional Conference where genuine representatives of the people of Zimbabwe as a whole would be able to work out a settlement relating to the future of the Territory;

9. Calls upon the Government of the United Kingdom to take all effective measures to bring about the conditions necessary to enable the people of Zimbabwe to exercise freely and fully their right to self-determination and independence including:

(a) The unconditional release of all political prisoners, detainees and restrictees;

(b) The repeal of all repressive and discriminatory legislation;

(c) The removal of all restrictions on political activity and the establishment of full democratic freedom and equality of political rights;

10. Decides to meet again and consider further actions in the light of future developments.

Resolution 333 (1973)
Adopted by the Security Council at its 1716th meeting
on 22 May 1973

The Security Council,

Recalling its resolutions 320 (1972) and 328 (1973),

Noting that measures so far instituted by the Security Council and the General Assembly have not brought to an end the illegal regime in Southern Rhodesia,

Reiterating its grave concern that some States, contrary to Security Council resolutions 232 (1966), 253 (1968) and 277 (1970) and to their obligations under Article 25 of the Charter of the United Nations, have failed to prevent trade with the illegal regime of Southern Rhodesia,

Condemning the persistent refusal of South Africa and Portugal to co-operate with the United Nations in the effective observance and implementation of sanctions against Southern Rhodesia (Zimbabwe) in clear violation of the United Nations Charter,

Having considered the second special report of the Committee established in pursuance of resolution 253 (1968) (S/10920),

Taking note of the letter dated 27 April from the Chairman of the Special Committee on the Situation with regard to the Implementation of the Declaration on the Granting of Independence to Colonial Countries and Peoples (S/10923),

1. Approves the recommendations and suggestions contained in paragraphs 10 to 22 (S/10920) of the second special report of the Committee established in pursuance of resolution 253 (1968);

2. Requests the Committee, as well as all Governments, and the Secretary-General as appropriate, to take urgent action to implement the recommendations and suggestions referred to above;

3. Requests States with legislation permitting importation of minerals and other products from Southern Rhodesia to repeal it immediately;

4. Calls upon States to enact and enforce immediately legislation providing for imposition of severe penalties on persons natural or juridical that evade or commit breach of sanctions by:

(a) Importing any goods from Southern Rhodesia;

(b) Exporting any goods to Southern Rhodesia;

(c) Providing any facilities for transport of goods to and from Southern Rhodesia;

(d) Conducting or facilitating any transaction or trade that may enable Southern Rhodesia to obtain from or send to any country any goods or services;

(e) Continuing to deal with clients in South Africa, Angola, Mozambique, Guinea (Bissau) and Namibia after it has become known that the clients are re-exporting the goods or components thereof to Southern Rhodesia, or that goods received from such clients are of Southern Rhodesian origin;

5. Requests States, in the event of their trading with South Africa and Portugal, to provide that purchase contracts with those countries should clearly stipulate, in a manner legally enforceable, prohibition of dealing in goods of Southern Rhodesian origin; likewise, sales contracts with these countries should include a prohibition of resale or re-export of goods to Southern Rhodesia;

135

6. Calls upon States to pass legislation forbidding insurance companies under their jurisdiction from covering air flights into and out of Southern Rhodesia and individuals or air cargo carried on them;

7. Calls upon States to undertake appropriate legislative measures to ensure that all valid marine insurance contracts contain specific provisions that no goods of Southern Rhodesian origin or destined to Southern Rhodesia shall be covered by such contracts;

8. Calls upon States to inform the Committee of the Security Council on their present sources of supply and quantities of chrome, asbestos, nickel, pig iron, tobacco, meat and sugar, together with the quantities of these goods they obtained from Southern Rhodesia before the application of sanctions.

Resolution 1514 (XV)
Declaration on the granting of independence to
colonial countries and peoples

The General Assembly,

Mindful of the determination proclaimed by the peoples of the
world in the Charter of the United Nations to reaffirm faith in fundamental human rights, in the dignity and worth of the human person,
in the equal rights of men and women and of nations large and small
and to promote social progress and better standards of life in larger
freedom,

Conscious of the need for the creation of conditions of stability
and well-being and peaceful and friendly relations based on respect
for the principles of equal rights and self-determination of all peoples,
and of universal respect for, and observance of, human rights and
fundamental freedoms for all without distinction as to race, sex,
language or religion,

Recognizing the passionate yearning for freedom in all dependent peoples and the decisive role of such peoples in the attainment
of their independence,

Aware of the increasing conflicts resulting from the denial of
or impediments in the way of the freedom of such peoples, which
constitute a serious threat to world peace,

Considering the important role of the United Nations in assisting
the movement for independence in Trust and Non-Self-Governing
Territories,

Recognizing that the peoples of the world ardently desire the
end of colonialism in all its manifestations,

Convinced that the continued existence of colonialism prevents
the development of international economic cooperation, impedes the
social, cultural and economic development of dependent peoples and
militates against the United Nations ideal of universal peace,

Affirming that peoples may, for their own ends, freely dispose
of their natural wealth and resources without prejudice to any obligations arising out of international economic co-operation, based
upon the principle of mutual benefit, and international law,

Believing that the process of liberation is irresistible and ir-
reversible and that, in order to avoid serious crises, an end must
be put to colonialism and all practices of segregation and discrimination associated therewith,

Welcoming the emergence in recent years of a large number of dependent territories into freedom and independence, and recognizing the increasingly powerful trends towards freedom in such territories which have not yet attained independence,

Convinced that all peoples have an inalienable right to complete freedom, the exercise of their sovereignty and the integrity of their national territory,

Solemnly proclaims the necessity of bringing to a speedy and unconditional end colonialism in all its forms and manifestations;

And to this end

Declares that:

1. The subjection of peoples to alien subjugation, domination and exploitation constitutes a denial of fundamental human rights, is contrary to the Charter of the United Nations and is an impediment to the promotion of world peace and co-operation.

2. All peoples have the right to self-determination; by virtue of that right they freely determine their political status and freely pursue their economic, social and cultural development.

3. Inadequacy of political, economic, social or educational preparedness should never serve as a pretext for delaying independence.

4. All armed action or repressive measures of all kinds directed against dependent peoples shall cease in order to enable them to exercise peacefully and freely their right to complete independence, and the integrity of their national territory shall be respected.

5. Immediate steps shall be taken, in Trust and Non-Self-Governing Territories or all other territories which have not yet attained independence, to transfer all powers to the peoples of those territories, without any conditions or reservations, in accordance with their freely expressed will and desire, without any distinction as to race, creed or colour, in order to enable them to enjoy complete independence and freedom.

6. Any attempt aimed at the partial or total disruption of the national unity and the territorial integrity of a country is incompatible with the purposes and principles of the Charter of the United Nations.

7. All States shall observe faithfully and strictly the provisions of the Charter of the United Nations, the Universal Declaration of Human Rights and the present Declaration on the basis of equality, noninterference in the internal affairs of all States, and respect for the sovereign rights of all peoples and their territorial integrity.

947th plenary meeting,
14 December 1960.

Resolution 1745 (XVI)
General questions relating to the transmission and examination of information from Non-Self-Governing Territories

The General Assembly,

Recalling resolution 1514 (XV) of 14 December 1960 entitled "Declaration on the granting of independence to colonial countries and peoples,"

Recalling its resolution 742 (VIII) of 27 November 1953, by which the General Assembly approved a list of factors to be used as a guide in determining whether a territory is or is not within the scope of Chapter XI of the Charter of the United Nations, and in particular section C of the second part of that list,

Recalling further resolution 1541 (XV) of 15 December 1960, by which the General Assembly approved a list of principles to be applied in the light of the facts and the circumstances of each case to determine whether or not an obligation exists to transmit information under Article 73 e of the Charter,

Bearing in mind that, according to principle XI set forth in resolution 1541 (XV), the constitution of a Non-Self-Governing Territory giving it self-government in economic and social matters has to be established through freely elected institutions,

Mindful of the fact that the indigenous inhabitants have not been adequately represented in the legislature and not represented at all in the government,

1. Requests the Special Committee established by General Assembly resolution 1654 (XVI) of 27 November 1961 to consider whether the territory of Southern Rhodesia has attained a full measure of self-government;

2. Requests the special Committee to report on this matter to the General Assembly at its seventeenth session.

1106th plenary meeting,
23 February 1962.

Resolution 1747 (XVI)
The question of Southern Rhodesia
(Resolution adopted without reference to a Committee)

The General Assembly,

Recalling its resolution 1514 (XV) of 14 December 1960 containing the Declaration on the granting of independence to colonial countries and peoples,

Having considered the report on the question of Southern Rhodesia submitted by the Special Committee on the Situation with regard to the Implementation of the Declaration on the Granting of Independence to colonial Countries and Peoples,

Considering that the vast majority of the people of Southern Rhodesia have rejected the Constitution of 6 December 1961,

Deploring the denial of equal political rights and liberties to the vast majority of the people of Southern Rhodesia,

Noting with regret that the Government of the United Kingdom of Great Britain and Northern Ireland has not yet taken steps to transfer all powers to the people of Southern Rhodesia, as required under paragraph 5 of resolution 1514 (XV),

Having further considered the evidence submitted by the petitioners before the Special Committee,

1. Approves the conclusions of the Special Committee on the Situation with regard to the Implementation of the Declaration on the Granting of Independence to colonial Countries and Peoples on Southern Rhodesia, and affirms that the Territory of Southern Rhodesia is a Non-Self-Governing Territory within the meaning of Chapter XI of the Charter of the United Nations;

2. Requests the Administering Authority:

(a) To undertake urgently the convening of a constitutional conference, in which there shall be full participation of representatives of all political parties, for the purpose of formulating a constitution for Southern Rhodesia, in place of the Constitution of 6 December 1961, which would ensure the rights of the majority of the people, on the basis of "one man, one vote", in conformity with the principles of the Charter of the United Nations and the Declaration on the granting of independence to colonial countries and peoples, embodied in General Assembly resolution 1514 (XV);

(b) To take immediate steps to restore all rights of the non-European population and remove all restraints and restrictions in law and in practice on the exercise of the freedom of political activity including all laws, ordinances and regulations which directly or indirectly sanction any policy or practice based on racial discrimination;

(c) To grant amnesty to, and ensure the immediate release of, all political prisoners;

3. Requests the Special Committee to continue its constructive efforts towards the earliest implementation of resolution 1514 (XV) with regard to Southern Rhodesia in order to ensure its emergence as an independent African State.

1121st plenary meeting,
28 June 1962.

Resolution 2012 (XX)
Question of Southern Rhodesia

The General Assembly,

Deeply concerned at the situation in Southern Rhodesia,

Noting with particular concern the repeated threats of the present authorities in Southern Rhodesia immediately to declare unilaterally the independence of Southern Rhodesia, in order to perpetuate
minority rule in Southern Rhodesia,

Noting the attitude of the Government of the United Kingdom of
Great Britain and Northern Ireland that a unilateral declaration of
independence for Southern Rhodesia would be an act of rebellion and
that any measure to give it effect would be an act of treason,

1. Condemns any attempt on the part of the Rhodesian authorities to seize independence by illegal means in order to perpetuate
minority rule in Southern Rhodesia;

2. Declares that the perpetuation of such minority rule would
be incompatible with the principle of equal rights and self-determination of peoples proclaimed in the Charter of the United Nations and
in the Declaration on the Granting of Independence to Colonial Countries and Peoples contained in General Assembly resolution 1514
(XV) of 14 December 1960;

3. Requests the United Kingdom of Great Britain and Northern
Ireland and all Member States not to accept a declaration of independence for Southern Rhodesia by the present authorities, which would
be in the sole interest of the minority, and not to recognize any authorities purporting to emerge therefrom;

4. Calls upon the United Kingdom to take all possible measures
to prevent a unilateral declaration of independence and, in the event
of such a declaration, to take all steps necessary to put an immediate
end to the rebellion, with a view to transferring power to a representative government in keeping with the aspirations of the majority
of the people;

5. Decides to keep the question of Southern Rhodesia under
urgent and continuing review during the twentieth session and to
consider what further steps may be necessary.
                        1357th plenary meeting,
                           12 October 1965.

Resolution 2022 (XX)
Question of Southern Rhodesia

The General Assembly,

Having examined the chapters of the reports of the Special
Committee on the Situation with regard to the Implementation of the

Declaration on the Granting of Independence to Colonial Countries and Peoples relating to Southern Rhodesia,

Recalling its resolutions 1514 (XV) of 14 December 1960, 1747 (XVI) of 28 June 1962, 1760 (XVII) of 31 October 1962, 1883 (XVIII) of 14 October 1963, 1889 (XVIII) of 6 November 1963, 1956 (XVIII) of 11 December 1963 and 2012 (XX) of 12 October 1965, the resolutions adopted by the Special Committee on 22 April 1965 and 28 May 1965, and Security Council resolution 202 (1965) of 6 May 1965,

Considering that the administering Power has not implemented the above resolutions and that no constitutional progress has been made,

Noting that the increasing co-operation between the authorities of Southern Rhodesia, South Africa and Portugal is designed to perpetuate racist minority rule in southern Africa and constitutes a threat to freedom, peace and security in Africa,

Noting with grave concern the manifest intention of the present authorities in Southern Rhodesia to proclaim independence unilaterally, which would continue the denial to the African majority of their fundamental rights to freedom and independence,

Deeply concerned about the explosive situation in Southern Rhodesia,

1. Approves the chapters of the reports of the Special Committee on the Situation with regard to the Implementation of the Declaration on the Granting of Independence to Colonial Countries and Peoples relating to Southern Rhodesia and endorses the conclusions and recommendations contained therein;

2. Reaffirms the right of the people of Southern Rhodesia to freedom and independence and recognizes the legitimacy of their struggle for the enjoyment of their rights as set forth in the Charter of the United Nations, the Universal Declaration of Human Rights and the Declaration on the Granting of Independence to Colonial Countries and Peoples contained in General Assembly resolution 1514 (XV);

3. Solemnly warns the present authorities in Southern Rhodesia and the United Kingdom of Great Britain and Northern Ireland, in its capacity as administering Power, that the United Nations will oppose any declaration of independence which is not based on universal adult suffrage;

4. Condemns the policies of racial discrimination and segregation practised in Southern Rhodesia, which constitute a crime against humanity;

5. Condemns any support or assistance rendered by any State to the minority regime in Southern Rhodesia;

6. Calls upon all States to refrain from rendering any assistance whatsoever to the minority regime in Southern Rhodesia;

7. *Requests* that the administering Power effect immediately;

(a) The release of all political prisoners, political detainees and restrictees,

(b) The repeal of all repressive and discriminatory legislation and, in particular, the Law and Order (Maintenance) Act and the Land Apportionment Act;

(c) The removal of all restrictions on African political activity and the establishment of full democratic freedom and equality of political rights;

8. *Requests once more* the Government of the United Kingdom to suspend the Constitution of 1961 and to call immediately a constitutional conference in which representatives of all political parties will take part, with a view to making new constitutional arrangements on the basis of universal adult suffrage and to fixing the earliest possible date for independence;

9. *Appeals* to all States to use all their powers against a unilateral declaration of independence and, in any case, not to recognize any government in Southern Rhodesia which is not representative of the majority of the people;

10. *Requests* all States to render moral and material help to the people of Zimbabwe in their struggle for freedom and independence;

11. *Calls upon* the Government of the United Kingdom to employ all necessary measures, including military force, to implement paragraphs 7 and 8 above;

12. *Draws the attention* of the Security Council to the threats made by the present authorities in Southern Rhodesia, including the threat of economic sabotage against the independent African States adjoining Southern Rhodesia;

13. *Further* draws the attention of the Security Council to the explosive situation in Southern Rhodesia which threatens international peace and security, and decides to transmit to the Council the records and resolutions of the twentieth session of the General Assembly on this question;

14. *Decides* to keep the question of Southern Rhodesia under urgent and continuing review.

1368th plenary meeting,
5 November 1965.

Resolution 2024 (XX)
Question of Southern Rhodesia

The General Assembly,

Considering the explosive situation created in Southern Rhodesia following the unilateral declaration of independence,

Noting the measures taken by the Government of the United Kingdom of Great Britain and Northern Ireland,

1. Condemns the unilateral declaration of independence made by the racialist minority in Southern Rhodesia;

2. Invites the United Kingdom of Great Britain and Northern Ireland to implement immediately the relevant resolutions adopted by the General Assembly and the Security Council in order to put an end to the rebellion by the unlawful authorities in Southern Rhodesia;

3. Recommends the Security Council to consider this situation as a matter of urgency.

1375th plenary meeting,
11 November 1965.

Resolution 2625 (XXV)
Declaration on Principles of International Law
concerning Friendly Relations and Co-operation
among States in accordance with the Charter of
the United Nations

The General Assembly,

Recalling its resolutions 1815 (XVII) of 18 December 1962, 1966 (XVIII) of 16 December 1963, 2103 (XX) of 20 December 1965, 2181 (XXI) of 12 December 1966, 2327 (XXII) of 18 December 1967, 2463 (XXIII) of 20 December 1968 and 2533 (XXIV) of 8 December 1969, in which it affirmed the importance of the progressive development and codification of the principles of international law concerning friendly relations and co-operation among States,

Having considered the report of the Special Committee on Principles of International Law concerning Friendly Relations and Co-operation among States, which met in Geneva from 31 March to 1 May 1970,

Emphasizing the paramount importance of the Charter of the United Nations for the maintenance of international peace and security and for the development of friendly relations and co-operation among States,

Deeply convinced that the adoption of the Declaration on Principles of International Law concerning Friendly Relations and Co-operation among States in accordance with the Charter of the United Nations on the occasion of the twenty-fifth anniversary of the United Nations would contribute to the strengthening of world peace and constitute a landmark in the development of international law and of relations among States, in promoting the rule of law among nations and particularly the universal application of the principles embodied in the Charter,

144

Considering the desirability of the wide dissemination of the text of the Declaration,

1. Approves the Declaration on Principles of International Law concerning Friendly Relations and Co-operation among States in accordance with the Charter of the United Nations, the text of which is annexed to the present resolution;

2. Expresses its appreciation to the Special Committee on Principles of International Law concerning Friendly Relations and Co-operation among States for its work resulting in the elaboration of the Declaration;

3. Recommends that all efforts be made so that the Declaration becomes generally known.

1883rd plenary meeting,
24 October 1970.

Annex
Declaration on Principles of International Law
concerning Friendly Relations and Co-operation among
States in accordance with the Charter of
the United Nations

Preamble

The General Assembly,

Reaffirming in the terms of the Charter of the United Nations that the maintenance of international peace and security and the development of friendly relations and co-operation between nations are among the fundamental purposes of the United Nations,

Recalling that the peoples of the United Nations are determined to practice tolerance and live together in peace with one another as good neighbors,

Bearing in mind the importance of maintaining and strengthening international peace founded upon freedom, equality, justice and respect for fundamental human rights and of developing friendly relations among nations irrespective of their political, economic and social systems or the levels of their development,

Bearing in mind also the paramount importance of the Charter of the United Nations in the promotion of the rule of law among nations,

Considering that the faithful observance of the principles of international law concerning friendly relations and co-operation among States and the fulfilment in good faith of the obligations assumed by States, in accordance with the Charter, is of the greatest importance for the maintenance of international peace and security and for the implementation of the other purposes of the United Nations,

Noting that the great political, economic and social changes and scientific progress which have taken place in the world since the adoption of the Charter give increased importance to these principles and to the need for their more effective application in the conduct of States wherever carried on,

Recalling the established principle that outer space, including the Moon and other celestial bodies, is not subject to national appropriation by claim of sovereignty, by means of use or occupation, or by any other means, and mindful of the fact that consideration is being given in the United Nations to the question of establishing other appropriate provisions similarly inspired,

Convinced that the strict observance by States of the obligation not to intervene in the affairs of any other State is an essential condition to ensure that nations live together in peace with one another, since the practice of any form of intervention not only violates the spirit and letter of the Charter, but also leads to the creation of situations which threaten international peace and security,

Recalling the duty of States to refrain in their international relations from military, political, economic or any other form of coercion aimed against the political independence or territorial integrity of any State,

Considering it essential that all States shall refrain in their international relations from the threat or use of force against the territorial integrity or political independence of any State, or in any other manner inconsistent with the purposes of the United Nations,

Considering it equally essential that all States shall settle their international disputes by peaceful means in accordance with the Charter,

Reaffirming, in accordance with the Charter, the basic importance of sovereign equality and stressing that the purposes of the United Nations can be implemented only if States enjoy sovereign equality and comply fully with the requirements of this principle in their international relations,

Convinced that the subjection of peoples to alien subjugation, domination and exploitation constitutes a major obstacle to the promotion of international peace and security,

Convinced that the principle of equal rights and self-determination of peoples constitutes a significant contribution to contemporary international law, and that its effective application is of paramount importance for the promotion of friendly relations among States, based on respect for the principle of sovereign equality,

Convinced in consequence that any attempt aimed at the partial or total disruption of the national unity and territorial integrity of a State or country or at its political independence is incompatible with the purposes and principles of the Charter,

Considering the provisions of the Charter as a whole and taking into account the role of relevant resolutions adopted by the competent organs of the United Nations relating to the content of the principles,

Considering that the progressive development and codification of the following principles:

(a) The principle that States shall refrain in their international relations from the threat or use of force against the territorial integrity or political independence of any State, or in any other manner inconsistent with the purposes of the United Nations,

(b) The principle that States shall settle their international disputes by peaceful means in such a manner that international peace and security and justice are not endangered,

(c) The duty not to intervene in matters within the domestic jurisdiction of any State, in accordance with the Charter,

(d) The duty of States to co-operate with one another in accordance with the Charter,

(e) The principle of equal rights and self-determination of peoples,

(f) The principle of sovereign equality of States,

(g) The principle that States shall fulfil in good faith the obligations assumed by them in accordance with the Charter, so as to secure their more effective application within the international community, would promote the realization of the purposes of the United Nations,

Having considered the principles of international law relating to friendly relations and co-operation among States,

1. Solemnly proclaims the following principles:

The principle that States shall refrain in their international relations from the threat or use of force against the territorial integrity or political independence of any State, or in any other manner inconsistent with the purposes of the United Nations

Every State has the duty to refrain in its international relations from the threat or use of force against the territorial integrity or political independence of any State, or in any other manner inconsistent with the purposes of the United Nations. Such a threat or use of force constitutes a violation of international law and the Charter of the United Nations and shall never be employed as a means of settling international issues.

A war of aggression constitutes a crime against the peace, for which there is responsibility under international law.

In accordance with the purposes and principles of the United Nations, States have the duty to refrain from propaganda for wars of aggression.

Every State has the duty to refrain from the threat or use of force to violate the existing international boundaries of another State or as a means of solving international disputes, including territorial disputes and problems concerning frontiers of States.

Every State likewise has the duty to refrain from the threat or use of force to violate international lines of demarcation, such as armistice lines, established by or pursuant to an international agreement to which it is a party or which it is otherwise bound to respect. Nothing in the foregoing shall be construed as prejudicing the positions of the parties concerned with regard to the status and effects of such lines under their special regimes or as affecting their temporary character.

States have a duty to refrain from acts of reprisal involving the use of force.

Every State has the duty to refrain from any forcible action which deprives peoples referred to in the elaboration of the principle of equal rights and self-determination of their right to self-determination and freedom and independence.

Every State has the duty to refrain from organizing or encouraging the organization of irregular forces or armed bands, including mercenaries, for incursion into the territory of another State.

Every State has the duty to refrain from organizing, instigating, assisting or participating in acts of civil strife or terrorist acts in another State or acquiescing in organized activities within its territory directed towards the commission of such acts, when the acts referred to in the present paragraph involve a threat or use of force.

The territory of a State shall not be the object of military occupation resulting from the use of force in contravention of the provisions of the Charter. The territory of a State shall not be the object of acquisition by another State resulting from the threat or use of force. No territorial acquisition resulting from the threat or use of force shall be recognized as legal. Nothing in the foregoing shall be construed as affecting:

(a) Provisions of the Charter or any international agreement prior to the Charter regime and valid under international law; or

(b) The powers of the Security Council under the Charter.

All States shall pursue in good faith negotiations for the early conclusion of a universal treaty on general and complete disarmament under effective international control and strive to adopt appropriate measures to reduce international tensions and strengthen confidence among States.

All States shall comply in good faith with their obligations under the generally recognized principles and rules of international law with respect to the maintenance of international peace and security, and shall endeavor to make the United Nations security system based on the Charter more effective.

Nothing in the foregoing paragraphs shall be construed as enlarging or diminishing in any way the scope of the provisions of the Charter concerning cases in which the use of force is lawful.

The principle that States shall settle their international disputes by peaceful means in such a manner that international peace and security and justice are not endangered

Every State shall settle its international disputes with other States by peaceful means in such a manner that international peace and security and justice are not endangered.

States shall accordingly seek early and just settlement of their international disputes by negotiation, inquiry, mediation, conciliation, arbitration, judicial settlement, resort to regional agencies or arrangements or other peaceful means of their choice. In seeking such a settlement the parties shall agree upon such peaceful means as may be appropriate to the circumstances and nature of the dispute.

The parties to a dispute have the duty, in the event of failure to reach a solution by any one of the above peaceful means, to continue to seek a settlement of the dispute by other peaceful means agreed upon by them.

States parties to an international dispute, as well as other States, shall refrain from any action which may aggravate the situation so as to endanger the maintenance of international peace and security, and shall act in accordance with the purposes and principles of the United Nations.

International disputes shall be settled on the basis of the sovereign equality of States and in accordance with the principle of free choice of means. Recourse to, or acceptance of, a settlement procedure freely agreed to by States with regard to existing or future disputes to which they are parties shall not be regarded as incompatible with sovereign equality.

Nothing in the foregoing paragraphs prejudices or derogates from the applicable provisions of the Charter, in particular those relating to the pacific settlement of international disputes.

The principle concerning the duty not to intervene in matters within the domestic jurisdiction of any State, in accordance with the Charter

No State or group of States has the right to intervene, directly or indirectly, for any reason whatever, in the internal or external affairs of any other State. Consequently, armed intervention and all other forms of interference or attempted threats against the personality of the State or against its political, economic and cultural elements, are in violation of international law.

No State may use or encourage the use of economic, political or any other type of measures to coerce another State in order to obtain from it the subordination of the exercise of its sovereign rights and to secure from it advantages of any kind. Also, no State shall organize, assist, foment, finance, incite or tolerate subversive, terrorist or armed activities directed towards the violent overthrow of the regime of another State, or interfere in civil strife in another State.

The use of force to deprive peoples of their national identity constitutes a violation of their inalienable rights and of the principle of non-intervention.

Every State has an inalienable right to choose its political, economic, social and cultural systems, without interference in any form by another State.

Nothing in the foregoing paragraphs shall be construed as affecting the relevant provisions of the Charter relating to the maintenance of international peace and security.

The duty of States to co-operate with one another in accordance with the Charter

States have the duty to co-operate with one another, irrespective of the differences in their political, economic and social systems, in the various spheres of international relations, in order to maintain international peace and security and to promote international economic stability and progress, the general welfare of nations and international co-operation free from discrimination based on such differences.

To this end:

(a) States shall co-operate with other States in the maintenance of international peace and security;

(b) States shall co-operate in the promotion of universal respect for, and observance of, human rights and fundamental freedoms for all, and in the elimination of all forms of racial discrimination and all forms of religious intolerance;

(c) States shall conduct their international relations in the economic, social, cultural, technical and trade fields in accordance with the principles of sovereign equality and non-intervention;

(d) States Members of the United Nations have the duty to take joint and separate action in co-operation with the United Nations in accordance with the relevant provisions of the Charter.

States should co-operate in the economic, social and cultural fields as well as in the field of science and technology and for the promotion of international cultural and educational progress. States should co-operate in the promotion of economic growth throughout the world, especially that of the developing countries.

The principle of equal rights and self-determination of peoples

By virtue of the principle of equal rights and self-determination of peoples enshrined in the Charter of the United Nations, all peoples have the right freely to determine, without external interference, their political status and to pursue their economic, social and cultural development, and every State has the duty to respect this right in accordance with the provisions of the Charter.

Every State has the duty to promote, through joint and separate action, realization of the principle of equal rights and self-determination of peoples, in accordance with the provisions of the Charter, and to render assistance to the United Nations in carrying out the responsibilities entrusted to it by the Charter regarding the implementation of the principle, in order:

(a) To promote friendly relations and co-operation among States; and

(b) To bring a speedy end to colonialism, having due regard to the freely expressed will of the peoples concerned; and bearing in mind that subjection of peoples to alien subjugation, domination and exploitation constitutes a violation of the principle, as well as a denial of fundamental human rights, and is contrary to the Charter.

Every State has the duty to promote through joint and separate action universal respect for and observance of human rights and fundamental freedoms in accordance with the Charter.

The establishment of a sovereign and independent State, the free association or integration with an independent State or the emergence into any other political status freely determined by a people constitute modes of implementing the right of self-determination by that people.

Every State has the duty to refrain from any forcible action which deprives peoples referred to above in the elaboration of the present principle of their right to self-determination and freedom and independence. In their actions against, and resistance to, such forcible action in pursuit of the exercise of their right to self-determination, such peoples are entitled to seek and to receive support in accordance with the purposes and principles of the Charter.

The territory of a colony or other Non-Self-Governing Territory has, under the Charter, a status separate and distinct from the territory of the State administering it; and such separate and distinct status under the Charter shall exist until the people of the colony or Non-Self-Governing Territory have exercised their right of self-determination in accordance with the Charter, and particularly its purposes and principles.

Nothing in the foregoing paragraphs shall be construed as authorizing or encouraging any action which would dismember or impair, totally or in part, the territorial integrity or political unity of sovereign and independent States conducting themselves in compliance with the principle of equal rights and self-determination of peoples as described above and thus possessed of a government representing the whole people belonging to the territory without distinction as to race, creed or colour.

Every State shall refrain from any action aimed at the partial or total disruption of the national unity and territorial integrity of any other State or country.

The principle of sovereign equality of States

All States enjoy sovereign equality. They have equal rights and duties and are equal members of the international community, notwithstanding differences of an economic, social, political or other nature.

In particular, sovereign equality includes the following elements:

(a) States are juridically equal;

(b) Each State enjoys the rights inherent in full sovereignty;

(c) Each State has the duty to respect the personality of other States;

(d) The territorial integrity and political independence of the State are inviolable;

(e) Each State has the right freely to choose and develop its political, social, economic and cultural systems;

(f) Each State has the duty to comply fully and in good faith with its international obligations and to live in peace with other States.

The principle that States shall fulfil in good faith the obligations assumed by them in accordance with the Charter

Every State has the duty to fulfil in good faith the obligations assumed by it in accordance with the Charter of the United Nations.

152

Every State has the duty to fulfil in good faith its obligations under the generally recognized principles and rules of international law.

Every State has the duty to fulfil in good faith its obligations under international agreements valid under the generally recognized principles and rules of international law.

Where obligations arising under international agreements are in conflict with the obligations of Members of the United Nations under the Charter of the United Nations, the obligations under the Charter shall prevail.

General Part

2. Declares that:

In their interpretation and application the above principles are interrelated and each principle should be construed in the context of the other principles.

Nothing in this Declaration shall be construed as prejudicing in any manner the provisions of the Charter or the rights and duties of Member States under the Charter or the rights of peoples under the Charter, taking into account the elaboration of these rights in this Declaration.

3. Declares further that:

The principles of the Charter which are embodied in this Declaration constitute basic principles of international law, and consequently appeals to all States to be guided by these principles in their international conduct and to develop their mutual relations on the basis of the strict observance of these principles.

APPENDIX C: IMPORTS FROM RHODESIA REPORTED TO THE
SECURITY COUNCIL SANCTIONS COMMITTEE
BY 75 NATIONS, 1965-72
(in thousands of U.S. dollars)

Importing Country*	1965	1966	1967	1968	1969	1970	1971	1972
United States	14,056[a]	9,359	6,463	1,599	68	115	807	12,400
Canada	3,152	1,087	4	2	1	1	2	5
Argentina	377	62	10	-	-	-	-	-
Brazil	55[a]	62	100	-	-	-	-	-
Chile	4[a]	-	-	-	-	-	-	-
Colombia	185	230	-	-	-	-	-	-
Mexico	2[a]	-	-	1[a]	-	-	-	-
Belgium-Luxembourg	2,806	3,540	1,998	829	477	142	97	10
France	2,873	1,856	1,059	1,171	50	61	130	907[b]
Germany, Federal Republic of	35,112	30,525	15,966	13,298	1,120	572	485	367
Italy	16,666	8,554	259	138	27	59	2	9
Netherlands	5,987	5,722	2,406	542	136	21	2	-
United Kingdom	83,711	12,809	405	215	163	117	129	222
Denmark	1,244	1,205	-	-	-	-	-	-
Norway	1,713	664	18	-	-	1	-	-
Sweden	1,960	182	-	-	-	-	-	1
Austria	4,436	1,673	249	95	26	-	-	-
Portugal	2,927[a]	2,148	5,635	3,582[c]	...	...	...	...
Switzerland[d]	5,678	4,155	3,925[e]	3,483[e]	3,625[e]	4,296[e]	4,511[e]	4,582[e]
Iceland	-	-	-	-	-	-	-	-
Ireland	967	142	70	32	4	-	-	-
Greece	2,581[a]	5,644[a]	677af 4[g]	-	-	-	10	...
Turkey	-	-	-	-	-	-	-	-
Spain	3,543	2,288	156	-	-	-	-	-
Finland	845	290	3	1	-	-	-	-
Yugoslavia	677[a]	-	-	-	-	-	-	-

Importing Country*	1965	1966	1967	1968	1969	1970	1971	1972
Jordan	-	470	201	20	11	. . .	. . .	-
Cyprus	398	260	2	2	1	1	1	-
Libyan Arab Republic	-	-	2	-	-	-	-	-
Israel	82[a]	-	-	-	-	-	. . .	. . .
Iran	244[a]	156	129	. . .	. . .	. . .	. . .	. . .
Lebanon	. . .	. . .	-	-	-	. . .	. . .	. . .
Egypt	1,241	189	1	12	94	-	. . .	-
Ethiopia	. . .	15	149	-	-	. . .	. . .	-
Australia	3,266	787	60	74	1	1	-	-
New Zealand	1,178	999	4	1	-	-	. . .	. . .
Botswana	5,432	. . .	826[h]	. . .	. . .	. . .	. . .	. . .
Uganda	561	25	-	. . .	. . .	. . .	. . .	. . .
Ghana	297	3	-	-	-	-	-	-
Mauritius	242	8	-	-	-	-	-	. . .
Nigeria	1,017[a]	507[a]	9	-	-	. . .	. . .	. . .
Zambia	99,507	64,904	45,129	31,602	30,481	32,473	29,429	25,719
Malawi	20,805	17,267	14,732	12,588	12,534	15,505	15,896[j]	21,077
Ivory Coast	-	-	-	-	-	-	. . .	. . .
Senegal	-	1	-	-	-	-	. . .	. . .
Angola	612[a]	689	1,137	374[i]	. . .	. . .	. . .	. . .
Mozambique	2,991	5,862	4,458	. . .	. . .	. . .	. . .	. . .
Liberia	5	9	9	-	. . .	. . .	. . .	. . .
Tunisia	236[a]	-	-	-	-	-	. . .	. . .
Japan	26,497	13,781	1,266	822	-	-	20	-
Ceylon	87	79	2	-	. . .	. . .	. . .	. . .
India	6,503	166	1	. . .	. . .	. . .	. . .	. . .
Pakistan	291[a]	-	-	-	-	-	. . .	. . .
Malaysia, West	3,569[a]	1,123	5	-	-	-	-	. . .

(continued)

Importing Country*	1965	1966	1967	1968	1969	1970	1971	1972
Singapore	2,109[a]	-	-	-	-	-	...	...
Sarawak	11[a]	2[a]	-	-	-	-	-	21
Brunei	-	-	-	-	-	-	...	...
Sabah	-	-	-	-	-	-	...	...
Hong Kong	2,313	2,082	22	-	-	-	-	-
Cambodia	88[a]	-	-	-	...	...	...	...
Laos	-	-	-	-	-	...	...	...
Viet-Nam, Republic of	-	-	-	78[a]	-	...	...	...
Indonesia	...	...	-	-	-	...	...	...
Korea, Republic of	-	-	-	-	-	-	-	...
Philippines	124[a]	335[a]	58[a]	-	-	...	...	...
Thailand	-	-	-	-	-	...	...	...
Jamaica	566[a]	456	-	-	...	...	...	...
Trinidad and Tobago	389	360	8	-	-	-	...	...
Barbados	22	-	-	-	-	...	...	...
Guyana	168	127	4	-	...	...	...	...
Netherlands Antilles	-	-	-	-	-	-	...	...
Fiji	222	125	38	-	_h	_c	...	...
Western Samoa	-	-	-	-	-	...	...	...
Malta	217	88	1	2	-	-	-	...

*Exports to the countries listed accounted for approximately 86 percent of the total exports of Southern Rhodesia in 1965 (pre-UDI).

[a]Refers to trade with the Federation of Rhodesia and Nyasaland.
[b]See Appendix F note.
[c]January-June.
[d]See the official declaration of the Swiss Government contained in document S/7781, Appendix B.
[e]"The Swiss importer is authorized to make use of his yearly quota any time of the year, e.g., in the early months of the year 1967. The quotas are compounded on the basis of the average import quantity of the commodity during the previous three years. Fluctuations are furthermore possible between the years, as the use of a yearly quota requested in December may only appear in the trade statistics of the first three months of the following year, the reason being that the import licenses granted within the quota are generally valid for three months."
[f]January-February.
[g]March-December.
[h]January-September.
[i]January-May.
[j]1971 figure has been recorded on a c.i.f. basis.

Source: Sixth Report of the Security Council Sanctions Committee, U.N. Document S/11178/Add. 2.

	1965	1966	1967	1968	1969	1970	1971	1972
South Africa Customs Union								
South African figures	1,008	1,127	1,310	1,458	1,446	1,422	1,414	1,811
23 reporting countries' figures[a]	1,060	1,210	1,401	1,589	1,668	1,674	1,640	2,128
Excess of imports over exports	52	83	91	131	222	252	226	317
Mozambique								
Mozambique figures	60	62	69	83	84	90	92	110[b]
23 reporting countries' figures[a]	81	81	120	137	124	150	141	200
Excess of imports over exports	21	19	51	54	40	60	49	90
Zambia								
Zambian figures	457	622	544	694	939	872	549	620
23 reporting countries' figures[a]	410	518	510	618	866	879	520	570
Excess of imports over exports	-47	-104	-34	-76	-73	7	-29	-34
Malawi								
Malawian figures	26	33	40	27	28	37	46	44
23 reporting countries' figures[a]	24	32	34	40	34	35	43	50
Excess of imports over exports	-2	-1	-6	13	6	-2	-3	2
Total								
Exporting countries' figures	1,551	1,844	1,963	2,262	2,497	2,417	2,101	2,585[b]
23 reporting countries' figures[a]	1,575	1,841	2,065	2,384	2,692	2,738	2,344	2,948
Excess of imports over exports	24	-3	102	122	195	317	243	363

[a]Reduced by 10 percent to cover freight etc.
[b]Estimated.

Source: Sixth Report of the Security Council Sanctions Committee, U.N. Document
S/11178/Add. 2.

Exporting Country*	1965	1966	1967	1968	1969	1970	1970	1972
United States	22,982a	7,491	3,757	2,024	455	514	652	700
Canada	3,625	575	89	22	2	16	-	17
Argentina	1	-	-	-	-	-	-	-
Brazil	86a	20	24	13	4	-	-	...
Chile	2a	-	-	-	-	...	...	...
Colombia	2	-	-	-	-	-	-	-
Mexico	207a	40a	103a	58a	6a	-	-	-
Belgium-Luxembourg	6,832	3,444	1,922	1,312	139	82	51	49
France	3,850	4,246	3,976	2,380	200	286	337	488
Germany, Federal Republic of	10,903	11,186	12,305	12,914	1,234	1,176	1,552	2,004
Italy	6,318	5,010	1,339	1,295	73	63	21	42
Netherlands	7,291	5,748	4,699	3,000	57	278	255	261
United Kingdom	88,808	7,648	2,877	1,946	1,958	1,206	1,698	1,796
Denmark	667	31	37	29	29	31	19	37
Norway	1,527	760	183	1	1	-	1	-
Sweden	3,413	51	1	-	2	-	-	-
Austria	800	1,256	1,252	1,082	87	-	-	-
Portugal	559a	1,055	1,824	878b	...	...	...	...
Switzerlandc	1,641	1,890	1,939	2,513	1,540	1,969	2,851	3,230
Iceland	-	-	1a	1a	-	-	-	-
Ireland	37	9	31	4	-	-	-	-
Greece	63a	19a	-	-	-	-	-	...
Turkey	2a	-	-	2	-	-	-	-
Spain	193	31	-	-	-	-	-	-
Finland	492	14	1	-	-	-	-	-
Yugoslavia	16a	81a	-	-	-	-	-	-
Jordan	-	-	-	-	-	-	-	-
Cyprus	5	3	4	1	1	1	1	-
Libyan Arab Republic	-	-	-	-	-	-	-	-
Israel	1,482a	-	-	-	5	-	-	...
Iran	2,821a	3	-	...	...	...	...	...
Lebanon	...	...	-	-	-	...	...	...
Egypt	1	-	-	-	-	-	...	-
Ethiopia	...	...	-	-	_d	...	...	-
Australia	4,510	4,072	5,653	5,851	3,539	4,937	4,840	4,060
New Zealand	237e	37e	7	12e	18e	-	-	...
Uganda	412	-	-	...	...	...	...	...
Ghana	17	-	2	-	-	-	-	-
Mauritius	6	-	-	-	-	-	-	...
Nigeria	129a	1,823a	6	-	-	...	...	...
Zambia	15,317	7,018	2,850	1,332	613	1,032	470	1,792
Malawi	4,359	2,951	2,735	2,872	3,804	5,148	5,315	4,297
Ivory Coast	-	-	-	-	-	-	...	...
Senegal	309a	122	-	-	...	...	...	...

Exporting Country*	1965	1966	1967	1968	1969	1970	1971	1972
Angola	304[a]	154	214	65[f]	. . .	. . .	. . .	. . .
Mozambique	3,247	2,698	3,818	. . .	. . .	. . .	. . .	. . .
Liberia	–	–	–	3	. . .	. . .	. . .	. . .
Tunisia	15[a]	26[a]	–	–	–	–	. . .	. . .
Japan	16,684	11,110	13,597	4,525	4	4	6	2
Ceylon	288	–	–	–	. . .	. . .	. . .	. . .
India	4,526	16	. . .	. . .	. . .	. . .	. . .	. . .
Pakistan	448[a]	–	–	–	–[g]	–	. . .	. . .
Malaysia, West	618[a]	12	–	–	–	–	–	. . .
Singapore	1,217[a]	–	–	–	–	–	–	. . .
Sarawak	–	–	–	–	–	–	–	. . .
Brunei	–	–	–	–	–	–	–	. . .
Sabah	–	–	–	–	–	–	. . .	. . .
Hong Kong	1,328	318	139	2	–	–	–	–
Cambodia	–	–	–	–	. . .	. . .	. . .	. . .
Laos	–	–	–	–	–	. . .	. . .	. . .
Viet-Nam, Republic of	–	–	–	–	–	–	. . .	. . .
Indonesia	. . .	. . .	–	. . .	–	. . .	. . .	. . .
Korea, Republic of	–	–	–	1	–	–	–	. . .
Philippines	2[a]	26[a]	3[a]	–	–	–	. . .	. . .
Thailand	–	–	–	–	–	. . .	. . .	. . .
Jamaica	2[a]	–	–	–[d]	. . .	. . .	. . .	. . .
Trinidad and Tobago	7	4	8	–	–	–	. . .	. . .
Barbados	–	–	–	–	–	. . .	. . .	. . .
Guyana	–	–	–	–	. . .	. . .	. . .	. . .
Netherlands Antilles	–	–	1	–	–	–	. . .	. . .
Fiji	–	–	–	–	–[h]	–[b]	. . .	. . .
Western Samoa	–	–	–	–	–	–	. . .	. . .
Malta	9	5	7	3	–	–	–	. . .

*Imports from the countries listed above accounted for approximately 75 percent of the total imports of Southern Rhodesia in 1965.

[a]Refers to trade with the Federation of Rhodesia and Nyasaland.
[b]January-June.
[c]See the official declaration of the Swiss Government contained in document S/7781, Appendix B.
[d]January-March.
[e]Domestic exports.
[f]January-May.
[g]July-December.
[h]January-September.

Source: Sixth Report of the Security Council Sanctions Committee, U.N. Document S/11178/Add. 2.

APPENDIX F: FIRST AND SECOND
SPECIAL REPORTS OF THE SANCTIONS COMMITTEE
ON THE IMPLEMENTATION OF SANCTIONS
(U.N. DOCUMENTS S/10632 AND S/10920)

Special Report of the Committee
Established in Pursuance of
Security Council Resolution 253 (1968)

I. Introduction

1. On 28 February 1972, in connection with the question concerning the situation in Southern Rhodesia, the Security Council
adopted resolution 314 (1972), paragraph 6 of which reads as follows:
"The Security Council, . . .

Requests the Committee established in pursuance of
Security Council resolution 253 (1968) to meet as a
matter of urgency to consider ways and means by which
the implementation of sanctions may be ensured and to
submit to the Security Council not later than 15 April
1972 a report containing recommendations in this respect, including any suggestions which the Committee
might wish to make concerning its terms of reference
and any other measures designed to ensure the effectiveness of its work, . . .

2. Since then, the Committee has held 38 meetings (64th to
101st, between 13 March and 8 May 1972).

II. Consideration by the Committee

3. In the course of the debate, some delegations suggested
that it would be useful if in the preparation of this special report
the Committee could benefit from the experience of other organs
or persons particularly competent in the matter. The Committee
therefore requested the Secretary-General to inquire whether the
Commonwealth Sanctions Committee (London) and the Sanctions and
Decolonization Section of the Organization of African Unity (Addis
Ababa) would be in a position to provide any comments which the
Committee might take into account in preparing its report. The
Committee received a preliminary reply from the Commonwealth

Secretary-General in his letter dated 11 April and noted that the matter would be placed before the Commonwealth Sanctions Committee at its next meeting. The Organization of African Unity sent an interim reply but was unable to provide its comments before the completion of this report.

4. Several delegations having presented or recalled proposals during their statements, the Committee was seized with four lists of concrete proposals submitted by the following delegations:

    (i) Guinea, Somalia and Sudan (proposals circulated on 7 April);

    (ii) Union of Soviet Socialist Republics (proposals circulated on 24 April);

    (iii) China (proposals circulated on 28 April);

    (iv) Guinea, Somalia and Sudan (supplementary proposals circulated on 4 May).

5. In view of the large number of proposals submitted to the Committee and of the need to communicate with other organs outside United Nations Headquarters, the Committee was obliged to seek from the Security Council an extension of the time-limit established in resolution 314 (1972) for the submission of its report. Subsequently the President of the Council informed the Committee that, following consultations among the members of the Council, there was no objection to the Committee's request to extend the time-limit first to 30 April and later to 8 May 1972.[1]

6. After detailed discussion of the four lists of proposals, the Committee agreed that the recommendations, suggestions and proposals reproduced in parts III (recommendations and suggestions) and IV (proposals) below should be included in the report. The recommendations and suggestions in part III as well as the content of paragraph 7 which follows have been accepted by all the delegations with the exception of that of the United Kingdom, which specifically requested that it be reported as having entered a blanket reservation on the recommendations, suggestions and proposals, as a whole, part III as well as part IV. It was not possible to reach agreement on the proposals in part IV and, consequently, it was agreed that each delegation might, if it so desired, have its position on those proposals briefly recorded.

III. Recommendations and Suggestions

7. The name of the Committee should be changed to "The Security Council Committee established in pursuance of resolution 253 (1968) concerning the question of Southern Rhodesia."

---

[1]See documents S/10597 and S/10622.

8. The Council will find in the following paragraphs recommendations on ways and means by which the implementation of sanctions may be ensured, suggestions concerning the terms of reference of the Committee and other measures designed to ensure the effectiveness of the work of the Committee.

9. Information from more Member States would be useful to the Committee. Only a very few Governments have reported up to now on cases of suspected violations. The Committee considers it essential that Members of the United Nations endeavor to bring cases of suspected sanctions evasions immediately to the notice of the Committee.

10. In addition to the information regarding suspected violations of sanctions brought to its notice by members and by the Secretariat, the Committee should also seek and may receive information in this connection from intergovernmental organizations and specialized agencies on a continuing basis.

11. The Committee should also invite, in accordance with rule 39 of the provisional rules of procedure of the Security Council, nongovernmental international organizations concerned with matters within its competence and all persons whom it considers competent for the purpose to supply it with information, or to give it other assistance and co-operation as the Committee may deem appropriate in the fulfilment of its tasks.

12. Governments should co-operate fully with the Committee in providing it with the information or other forms of assistance and co-operation obtained from all suitable sources in their territories, including natural and juridical persons within their jurisdiction, which are necessary for the discharge of its tasks.

13. The Secretariat of the Committee should be in a position to keep the Committee continuously and adequately informed of all developments relevant to the task entrusted to it by Security Council resolutions 253 (1968), 277 (1970) and 314 (1972). It should also initiate any specialized studies required by the Committee with the assistance, when necessary, of other competent departments of the Secretariat.

14. Information from published sources including press reports regarding suspected violations of sanctions should be circulated to all members without delay. The information would be placed before the next meeting of the Committee so as to enable the Committee to consider any appropriate action that might be required.

15. Governments should be urged to give prompt attention to requests for information from the Committee.

16. The Committee decided accordingly to request Governments to reply within a stated period depending on the particular circumstances of each case and in any event not later than two months.

If at the end of that period no reply has been received, and two reminders fail to elicit a response, the Committee should consider all necessary and appropriate measures to ensure compliance with its requests including referral of the case to the Security Council. The interval at which reminders ought to be dispatched will be determined by the Committee according to the nature of each case but in no case will it exceed one month.

17. The Committee should meet not less than twice a month and in urgent cases it should convene at the request of any member.

18. As part of the need of keeping the international community regularly informed, the Committee should, at the end of each meeting, consider the issuance of a press release covering its work and matters of topical interest including those cases where infringement of sanctions has been established or prevented.

19. In view of the announced refusal of South Africa and Portugal to co-operate with the Security Council in the implementation of sanctions, documentation emanating from South Africa and from the Portuguese controlled Territories of Mozambique and Angola in respect of products and goods which are also produced by Southern Rhodesia should be considered prima facie suspect. For purposes of investigation, therefore, the Committee should request all Governments to exercise closer scrutiny of such documents and to conduct an actual examination of cargoes to ensure that they are not of Southern Rhodesian origin.

20. In view of the large-scale falsification of commercial documents for goods originating from Southern Rhodesia, the Committee decided that it would resume its studies on this matter and that it should request expert advice to assist in the examination and devising of additional measures for preventing the circumvention of sanctions.

21. For the Committee to be able to fulfil its duties of examining the reports of the Secretary-General on the implementation of Security Council resolutions 253 (1968) and 277 (1970), and to submit, when necessary, its observations thereon to the Security Council, the Secretary-General should be invited to submit such reports more frequently, if possible quarterly, including periodic statistics of foreign trade.

22. The Committee should actively pursue all its responsibilities as provided by subparagraph 20 (b) of resolution 253 (1968)[1]

---

[1]Subparagraph 20 (b) of resolution 253 (1968) reads as follows:

"To seek from any States Members of the United Nations or of the specialized agencies such further information regarding the trade of that State (including information regarding the commodities and products exempted from the prohibition contained in operative paraas well as by subparagraph 21 (b) of resolution 277 (1970).[1]

23. Bearing in mind the need to keep the Security Council more frequently informed, the Committee should endeavor to submit quarterly reports to the Security Council. The Committee will, in the light of its experience, review this practice after a year's time and decide whether it is appropriate to adhere to it. The Committee will also submit to the Council interim reports when it considers this necessary.

24. The Committee attaches great importance to the question of the insurance of all cargoes of Southern Rhodesian origin and of all cargoes destined to Southern Rhodesia together with the question of the insurance of ships, aircraft, road and rail transport involved in the conveyance of those cargoes. With the aim of being able to adopt any necessary measures in this field, the Committee should request the Secretary-General to make available without delay the necessary expert advice which would clarify the role of insurance companies and indicate, where possible, those areas where, with the co-operation of such companies, the United Nations would be able to improve the effectiveness of sanctions.

IV. Proposals

Proposals submitted by the delegations of
Guinea, Somalia and Sudan

25. The Security Council should reaffirm the inalienable rights of the people of Southern Rhodesia to freedom and independence in accordance with the Declaration on the Granting of Independence to Colonial Countries and Peoples contained in General Assembly resolution 1514 (XV) of 14 December 1960, and the legitimacy of their struggle to secure the enjoyment of their rights as set forth in the Charter of the United Nations.

---

graph 3 (d) above) or regarding any activities by any nationals of that State or in its territories that may constitute an evasion of the measures decided upon in this resolution as it may consider necessary for the proper discharge of its duty to report to the Security Council."

[1]Subparagraph 21 (b) of resolution 277 (1970) reads as follows:

"Seeking from Member States such further information regarding the effective implementation of the provisions laid down in the present resolution as it may consider necessary for the proper discharge of its duty to report to the Security Council."

26. The Security Council should request States continuing to have economic and other relations with Southern Rhodesia to end such relations immediately. All States which are openly and persistently violating the provisions of Security Council resolutions 253 (1968) and 277 (1970) should be condemned. The Council should also request that member States, especially the permanent members of the Security Council, should reaffirm their obligations to fully implement these resolutions as they are called upon to do in paragraph 16 of resolution 253 (1968).

27. The Security Council should undertake as a matter of urgency consideration of the type of action to be taken in view of the open and persistent refusal of South Africa and Portugal to implement sanctions against the illegal regime of Southern Rhodesia and to co-operate with the Security Council on this matter.

28. The Security Council should now call upon all States to employ against the illegal regime in Southern Rhodesia additional measures provided for in Article 41 of the Charter as envisaged in paragraphs (9) of resolution 253 (1968) and (9) and (11) of resolution 277 (1970).

Positions of delegations concerning the
above proposals

29. In addition to the three sponsors, the following delegations have expressed their support for those proposals: Argentina, China, India, Panama, USSR and Yugoslavia.

30. The representative of China stressed that his delegation maintained its stand that the Committee should recommend to the Security Council to condemn the United States Government for violating the sanctions against Southern Rhodesia and to extend the sanctions to cover South Africa and Portugal.

31. The representative of Japan expressed its sympathy and support in principle for the objective and substance of the African proposals. However, Japan reserved its position in the Committee for procedural reasons and did not associate itself with the African proposals.

32. The representative of the Soviet Union noted that his delegation would prefer to have the Committee recommend to the Security Council that it should condemn the United States for open violation of the sanctions and that it should extend the sanctions to South Africa and Portugal, as was proposed by the Soviet delegation in its concrete proposals of 24 April.

33. The delegations of Belgium, France, Italy and the United States of America expressed the view that, while general agreement had been reached on the body of the Committee's report in response to Security Council resolution 314 (1972), it was not possible for them

to agree to the proposals submitted on 4 May by the African members
of the Committee. In their opinion the proposals were similar to
those which had been submitted earlier in the Committee and had
given rise to objections either to the substance, to the procedure
or to competence of the Committee in matters exclusively reserved
to the Security Council. Those objections remained valid with respect
to the supplementary proposals. Their objections were without prejudice to the position their delegations may take in the Security Council.

34. In proposing paragraph 26 the African countries took cog-
nizance of the fact that the United States was in open contravention
of resolutions 253 (1968) and 277 (1970) following its decision to
permit the importation of chrome ore from Southern Rhodesia. However, since the matter is the subject of an interim report to the
Security Council, the three African delegations decided to express
their position in greater detail when that report is taken up by the
Council.

Second Special Report of the Committee Established in
Pursuance of Security Council Resolution 253 (1968)
Concerning the Question of Southern Rhodesia

I. Introduction

1. On 29 September 1972, in connection with the question
concerning the situation in Southern Rhodesia, the Security Council
adopted resolution 320 (1972), paragraphs 4 and 5 of which read as
follows:

> 4. Requests the Security Council Committee established
> in pursuance of resolution 253 (1968) concerning the
> Question of Southern Rhodesia to undertake, as a matter
> of urgency, consideration of the type of action which
> could be taken in view of the open and persistent re-
> fusal of South Africa and Portugal to implement sanc-
> tions against the illegal regime in Southern Rhodesia
> (Zimbabwe) and to report to the Council not later than
> 31 January 1973;
> 5. Further requests the Committee to examine and sub-
> mit a report to the Security Council not later than 31 Jan-
> uary 1973 on all proposals and suggestions made at the
> 1663rd to 166th meetings of the Council for extending the
> scope and improving the effectiveness of sanctions against
> Southern Rhodesia (Zimbabwe).

166

2. Since then, the Committee has held 26 meetings (115th to 140th).

II. Consideration by the Committee

3. At the 121st meeting on 8 February 1973, the representative of Sudan, on behalf of his own delegation and those of Guinea and Kenya, submitted a working paper entitled "Proposals on the implementation of operative paragraphs 4 and 5 of Security Council resolution 320 (1972)."

4. The Committee decided to take this paper as a basis for its discussions. It was also decided that the 24 proposals which it contained would be discussed by grouping them by subject.

5. In the course of the debate, a number of proposals were submitted by other delegations. The Committee also received various analyses and other working papers prepared by the Secretariat.

6. In view of the number and the scope of the proposals submitted to it, the Committee was compelled to request the Security Council to extend the time-limit indicated in resolution 320 (1972) for the submission of its report. Subsequently, the President of the Council informed the Committee that following consultations with the members of the Security Council, it had been agreed that the time-limit be extended first to 28 February and later to 15 April 1973.[1]

7. At its 135th meeting, the Committee interviewed Mr. Carl McDowell, President of the American Institute of Underwriters and his assistant, Mr. Roy Leifflen who appeared as expert consultant, regarding the question of marine insurance.

8. With a view to reconciling the various proposals before the Committee, a drafting group was established at the 134th meeting on 28 March. The following members were nominated to take part in its work: Australia, Indonesia, Panama, the Union of Soviet Socialist Republics, the Sudan, the United Kingdom and Yugoslavia. It was agreed, however, that, if they so wished, other delegations could join the group. The drafting group held eight meetings under the chairmanship of Indonesia. Its report was submitted to the Committee on 10 April 1973 at the 136th meeting.

9. After detailed discussion of the proposals submitted to it, the Committee agreed that the recommendations, suggestions and proposals reproduced in sections III (recommendations and suggestions) and IV (proposals) below should be included in the report.

---

[1]See documents S/10873 and S/10890.

The recommendations and suggestions in section III have been accepted by all the delegations. It was not possible to reach agreement on the proposals in section IV and, consequently, it was agreed that each delegation might, if it so desired, have its position on those proposals briefly recorded.

III. Recommendations and Suggestions

10. The Committee recalled Security Council resolution 318 (1972) approving the recommendation of the Committee contained in paragraph 19 of its first special report (S/10632), according to which documentation emanating from South Africa and from the Portuguese-controlled Territories of Mozambique and Angola in respect of products and goods that are also produced by Southern Rhodesia should be considered prima facie suspect. Accordingly, the Committee recommends that all States that have not already done so should be requested to institute urgently effective procedures at the point of importation to ensure that such goods arriving for importation from South Africa, Mozambique and Angola are not cleared through customs until they are satisfied that the documentation is adequate and complete and to ensure that such procedures provide for the recall of cleared goods to customs custody if subsequently established to be of Southern Rhodesian origin.

11. To assist States in making such procedures more effective, the Committee should urgently produce a manual setting forth documentation and clearing procedures necessary to determine the true origin of products that are known to be produced in Southern Rhodesia particularly chrome ore, asbestos, tobacco, pig iron, copper, sugar, maize and meat products and establishing guidelines for confiscation in the appropriate cases (as referred to in paragraph 14 below).

12. To assist Governments in their efforts to prevent violations of sanctions, the Committee should publish a list of experts whose names will have been put forward to the Committee by Governments and who would be available to be called in at short notice, with the consent of their Governments in the case of Government employees, by the Government of any importing country, which will normally bear the expenses, to make appropriate investigation. The Committee may also offer to any Government of an importing country the assistance of one or more experts to investigate cargo on the spot.

13. The Committee recommends to the Council that Member States, as well as the Committee, should, by taking adequate measures, encourage individuals and non-governmental organizations to report to the concerned bodies reliable information regarding sanctions-breaking operations.

14. The Committee recommends that all Member States should seize, in accordance with their domestic regulations, especially those based on relevant Security Council resolutions, cargoes established to be of Rhodesian origin that have been imported or have arrived for importation into their country.

15. The Committee recommends the establishment of a special fund, which should be financed by voluntary contributions, especially the equivalent of the proceeds of the sales of goods seized as recommended in paragraph 14 above. This fund should be used to the extent possible for the payment of expenses of experts referred to in paragraph 12 above when they are called in and the implementation of measures referred to in paragraph 13 above. In addition, the Committee might also make appropriations for other purposes consistent with resolution 253 (1968) if funds are available.

16. The Committee thinks that awareness on the part of Member States of the whole purpose of the United Nations sanctions policy is vital and, therefore, that it should periodically request Member States to draw the attention of their public to the importance of the relevant United Nations resolutions.

17. The Committee recommends that Member States, especially those with extensive consular services in southern Africa, should be urged to assist the Committee in the collection of information on sanctions violations, so as to increase the amount of such information available to the Committee.

18. The Committee should release quarterly lists containing names of:

(a) Companies found guilty of sanctions violations;

(b) Governments that have not responded within the prescribed period of two months to an inquiry from the Committee regarding cases in question, including the names of any companies involved.

19. The Committee, recalling paragraph 13 of its special report to the Security Council (S/10632) of 9 May 1972 and noting that its volume of work has greatly increased since the approval of that report by the Security Council, recommends that the team within the Secretariat that services the Committee should be reinforced, so as to enable it to keep the Committee continuously and adequately informed of developments relative to its task as entrusted to it by the relevant Security Council resolutions. In particular, the Committee recommends the appointment within this team of an individual with experience of international commerce, particularly of trade conducted through third parties, who would be responsible to the Committee, attend all meetings of the Committee, take any necessary action, including publicity action, at the Committee's request, make suggestions to the Committee and prepare work for the Committee, including, where appropriate, the submission to it

of draft notes to Governments requesting further clarification or explanation.

20. The Committee should circulate lists of all goods that Rhodesia is currently known to export, with comparable up-to-date lists of similar exports from South Africa, Mozambique and Angola, to establish the extent to which the South African, Mozambique and Angola exports have increased since the unilateral declaration of independence.

21. The Committee noted the flagrant and widespread violations of sanctions demonstrated by, in addition to other evidence, the discrepancies, in particular those revealed in annex V of its fifth report (S/10852/Add. 2), between the quantities of certain commodities reported to have been imported from South Africa, Mozambique and Angola and the quantities reported to have been exported by those countries. The Committee proposes that the Secretary-General should write to the representatives of all States trading with South Africa, Mozambique and Angola, with a copy to other Member States for information, drawing their attention to the existence of these discrepancies, to the Secretary-General's memorandum on the application of sanctions of 18 September 1969 and to the Secretary-General's note of 27 July 1971 regarding documentation necessary for importing from and exporting to Mozambique. The Secretary-General should request their comments on the discrepancies, in so far as they concern their countries. He should also request information on the precautions they are taking, bearing in mind the Secretary-General's communications referred to above, to ensure that products, in particular chrome ore, asbestos, tobacco, pig iron, copper, sugar, maize and meat products, purporting to originate in South Africa, Mozambique and Angola and now imported in greater quantities than in 1965, in fact originate in these territories and are not disguised Rhodesian exports. The Committee proposes that the Secretary-General's notes and the replies of Governments should be published.

22. The Committee recommends to the Council that the Member States should be requested to inform the Committee in three months' time of the action that they have taken or intended to take with respect to the recommendations contained in paragraphs 10, 13, 14, 16, 17 and 21.

IV. Proposals Submitted by the African Delegations
(Guinea, Kenya, and Sudan) and Alternative
Proposals Submitted by Other Delegations

23. (a) African proposal. The Committee should recommend that the Security Council decide that all States should limit their

purchases of chromium ores, asbestos, tobacco, pig iron, copper, sugar, maize and meat products from South Africa, Mozambique and Angola to the levels (in quantity) prevailing in 1965.

(b) USSR proposal.

(i) The Committee should recommend that the Security Council decide that all States should cease their purchases of chromium ores, asbestos, tobacco, pig iron, copper, sugar, maize and meat products from South Africa, Mozambique and Angola;

(ii) The Committee should recommend to the Security Council that it institute an obligatory embargo on the sale to South Africa and Portugal of petroleum and petroleum products;

(iii) The Committee should recommend to the Security Council that it institute an obligatory embargo on the delivery to South Africa and Portugal of all types of arms, military equipment, material and munitions.

(iv) The Committee should recommend that the Security Council decide that all States should take all measures against Southern Rhodesia in accordance with Article 41 of the Charter, including complete interruption of radio, telephone, telegraphic, postal and other means of communication.

24. (a) African proposal. Member States should be requested to require that purchase contracts for goods from South Africa and the Portuguese Territories should include a clause to the effect that if goods purporting to be from those Territories turn out to be of Rhodesian origin, this would automatically render the contract void.

(b) United Kingdom proposal. The Committee should recommend that Governments whose domestic legislation or regulations do not enable them to take action against their nationals and companies who seek to evade sanctions by

(i) Importing goods from Southern Rhodesia without declaring their true point of origin,

(ii) Exporting goods for resale to Southern Rhodesia, or

(iii) Continuing to supply goods to customers in South Africa and the Portuguese Territories after it has become known to them that the customers are re-exporting the goods to Rhodesia should be requested to enact and enforce adequate legislation or regulations as soon as possible.

(c) United States proposal. The Committee should recommend to the Council that all States should impose legal penalties on their nationals who seek to evade sanctions by importing goods from Southern Rhodesia without declaring their true point of origin.

25. (a) African proposal. The Committee should recommend to the Council that Member States should be requested to require that sales contracts between their countries and South Africa and the Portuguese Territories—especially for such goods as aircraft,

vehicles, machinery spare parts etc—should include a clause expressly forbidding any resale to Rhodesia and a clause to the effect that further sales would be prohibited should the condition be broken.

(b) French proposal. The Committee should recommend to the Council that Member States should be requested to invite the suppliers to guard against the danger of illegal re-exportation by requesting their customers to supply a certificate forbidding re-exportation to Southern Rhodesia.

(c) United Kingdom proposal. The Committee should recommend that Governments should be requested to discuss with their importers and exporters whether there are any effective and practical precautionary steps that exporters and importers could take in order to achieve more effective application of existing sanctions measures.

(d) United States proposal. The Committee should recommend to the Council that Member States should be requested to establish requirements that would forbid any resale to Southern Rhodesia of any export sales between their countries and South Africa and the Portuguese Territories, especially of such goods as aircraft vehicles and machinery spare parts.

26. The African delegations also proposed that the Committee should recommend that the Security Council decide that all States should deny landing rights to the national carriers of countries which continued to grant landing rights to aircraft from Southern Rhodesia or operate air services to Southern Rhodesia.

27. The Committee also should recommend that the Council request Member States to pass legislation to forbid insurance companies from covering air flights into or out of Southern Rhodesia.

28. It should also recommend that the Council call upon Member States to enact legislation creating impediments to the sale and transport of Rhodesian goods or of goods destined for Southern Rhodesia, specifying that no shipping lines should carry any such goods and that insurance companies should not insure such goods or ships carrying them.

29. The Committee should recommend to the Council that Member States legislate or otherwise provide that insurance companies attach warranties to all marine insurance contracts specifying that no goods of Southern Rhodesian origin are covered by the contract.

30. The United Kingdom submitted the following as an alternative proposal to paragraphs 27, 28 and 29:

The Committee should recommend that Governments should be requested to discuss with their insurance industries whether there are any practical and effective precautionary measures that insurers, whether of cargoes or of hulls (ship and aircraft), could take in order to achieve more effective application of existing sanctions measures.

31. The African delegations further proposed that the Committee should recommend to the Council that the Beira blockade should be extended to cover Lourenço Marques and that the blockade should be extended to cover commodities and products originating from Southern Rhodesia.

32. The Committee should recommend to the Security Council that the Council should inquire from Member States whether they would be willing to join with the British Navy in patrolling Beira.

33. The Committee should recommend that the United States should be requested to co-operate fully with the United Nations in the effective implementation of sanctions and to revoke its existing legislation permitting the importation of minerals from Southern Rhodesia.

34. The Committee should call upon all Member States to inform it as to their present sources of supply for chrome, asbestos, nickel, pig iron, tobacco, meat and sugar that they used to obtain from Southern Rhodesia before the application of sanctions.

V. Positions of Delegations

35. The delegation of Australia would have been able to support more of the African proposals than had been adopted and would have liked to see some of the proposals which had been adopted put in a stronger form. It regretted the situation that had necessitated the report, namely the failure of a number of States to carry out their obligations under Security Council resolution 253 (1968).

36. The Austrian delegation wished to state that it fully agreed with the intent and the spirit of the African proposals as a whole and that it could have supported a number of those proposals on which there was no agreement in the Committee, either in their original forms or with minor modifications that would not have derogated from their objectives. On some proposals, however, the Austrian delegation was unable to agree, as it considered them incompatible with Austria's domestic legal order. Nevertheless, the Austrian delegation earnestly hoped that further agreement could be reached at a later stage, once a thorough discussion had led to a fuller appreciation of the highly complex legal and technical problems involved.

37. The delegation of China stated that, in view of the fact that the South African authorities and the Portuguese Government had long violated the sanctions against Southern Rhodesia by every means, the Security Council should adopt resolutions to expand the sanctions to cover South Africa and Portugal. The Chinese delegation supported the proposals submitted by the African countries as preliminary measures to strengthen sanctions against Southern Rhodesia.

38. The delegation of France stated that it was in favor of the recommendations, the purpose of which was to strengthen the sanctions. In its view, practical measures for applying the sanctions should be considered, on the basis that the prime criterion for such measures must be their effectiveness. It was from that standpoint that it had endorsed the paragraphs contained in section III.

39. With regard to the paragraphs on which it had not been possible to reach a consensus, France wished to observe that it had no objections of principle concerning paragraphs 28, 29, 33 and 34.

40. The delegations of Guinea, Kenya and the Sudan stated that a number of replies given to the Committee by Mr. Carl McDowell and Mr. Roy Leifflen, who, on its invitation, had appeared before the Committee at its 135th meeting on 3 April 1973 and answered Committee members' questions, confirmed that the African proposals in paragraphs 27, 28 and 29 were realistic and necessary, that the action envisaged would be possible and would constitute an important contribution to the sanctions' effectiveness.

41. The delegations of Guinea, Kenya and the Sudan accepted the proposals submitted by the delegations of the People's Republic of China and the USSR. Those proposals reflected fully the African position. If the African delegations had not put forward those same views in their original proposals to the Committee, it was only because it was felt that there existed room for accommodation of various views and points of interest. The African proposals were therefore the bare minimum requirements.

42. The delegations of Guinea, Kenya and the Sudan continued to believe that it was South Africa and Portugal that were mainly responsible for Security Council sanctions violation.

43. The African delegations would therefore continue to press such views in the Security Council and to seek measures to extend sanctions to cover South Africa and Portugal.

44. Having fully supported the proposals of the delegations of Guinea, Kenya and the Sudan, as submitted to the Committee and adopted as the basic working paper for the Committee's work on the second special report, the following delegations would continue to support the African proposals and positions contained in section IV of the report: India, Indonesia, Panama, Peru and Yugoslavia.

45. The delegation of Indonesia believed that it had, in a very modest way, contributed to the formulation of the proposals as they appeared in the African working paper. Those proposals, as they stood, would be adequate for the purpose of putting effective pressures on those countries which did not pay heed to the various Security Council resolutions on sanctions. As such, those proposals had the all-out support of the Indonesian delegation, which would have been happy indeed if those proposals could have been accepted in their

entirety by the Committee. That, however, had proved impossible. The delegation of Indonesia had also contributed in a modest manner to the work of the drafting group that had been entrusted by the Committee to locate possible areas of agreement as well as those areas where agreement was not possible.

46. The report produced by the drafting group had presented some formulas that could be agreed upon in principle by the drafting group. The delegation of Indonesia was not completely satisfied with those agreed formulas, since they did not seem to be adequate enough for the purposes mentioned in paragraph 4 of resolution 320 (1972). None the less, for the sole purpose of achieving unanimity, the Indonesian delegation was prepared to support the proposals that had been agreed upon by the whole Committee.

47. With regard to those proposals that were in the unagreed portion, the Indonesian delegation wished to express its support for the text in the original African working paper. The various amendments to those original proposals were unacceptable to the Indonesian delegation.

48. When the African document had been introduced by the representative of the Sudan, the delegation of Peru had expressed its agreement with the measures proposed therein. During the consideration of those proposals by the Committee, it had been found impossible to reach unanimous agreement on all of them, and the proposals on which there was no agreement had therefore been included in section IV of the Committee's report. Faced with that situation, the delegation of Peru reaffirmed its support for the proposals of the African countries. In Section IV of the report, it considered that paragraphs 23 (a), 24 (a) and 25 (a) referred to specific situations which were in fact at the center of the problem of sanctions violations. Paragraph 23 (a) referred to a specific aspect of the problem, namely the export of goods of Southern Rhodesian origin through South Africa and the Territories under Portuguese administration; the Peruvian delegation was in agreement with the contents of that paragraph as it appeared in the African document. Paragraphs 24 (a) and 25 (a) contained very constructive suggestions for the avoidance of sanctions violations because the inclusion of clauses whereby purchase and sales contracts with South Africa and the Portuguese Territories would be rendered null and void if it was found that the goods involved were of Southern Rhodesian origin, and a clause prohibiting resale to Southern Rhodesia were effective measures which might well be considered in connexion with the internal legislation of countries.

49. Paragraphs 26, 27, 28 and 29 contained practicable proposals in that States could enact legislation forbidding insurance companies from covering goods of Southern Rhodesian origin,

especially since, in the opinion of the insurance expert consulted by the Committee, insurance companies knew the origin of the goods which they insured.

50. Lastly, the Peruvian delegation reaffirmed its agreement with the content of paragraphs 31, 32, 33 and 34 in section IV of the report.

51. The Soviet delegation stated that, in its view, the recommendations and proposals of the Committee to the Security Council contained in its report were inadequate from the point of view of discharging the mandate given to the Committee under Security Council resolution 320 (1972). They did not include either recommendations concerning the type of action which could be taken in view of the open and persistent refusal of South Africa and Portugal to implement sanctions against the illegal regime in Southern Rhodesia, as provided in that resolution, or recommendations for extending the scope of sanctions against Southern Rhodesia, as provided in that resolution.

52. The Soviet delegation to the Committee proposed that, in view of the fact that South Africa, as well as Angola and Mozambique which were under the colonial domination of Portugal, were the main gates through which illegal trade with Southern Rhodesia was carried on in violation of the Security Council sanctions the Committee should recommend in its report to the Security Council that all States should cease their purchases of chromium ores, asbestos, tobacco, pig iron, copper, sugar, maize and meat products, in other words of goods which were Southern Rhodesia's main exports, from South Africa, Mozambique and Angola; that an obligatory embargo should be instituted on the sale to South Africa and Portugal of petroleum and petroleum products; and that an obligatory embargo should be instituted on the delivery to South Africa and Portugal of all types of arms, military equipment, material and munitions.

53. The Soviet delegation proposed the following specific expansion of sanctions against Southern Rhodesia: that all States, in accordance with Article 41 of the Charter, should completely sever all radio, telephone, telegraphic, postal and other means of communication with Southern Rhodesia.

54. The Soviet delegation also supported the proposals along those lines submitted by the African countries which are members of the Committee.

55. The United Kingdom delegation stated that it shared what it understood to be the principal objective underlying the proposals originally put forward by the three African delegations, namely, that "in view of the open persistent refusal of South Africa and Portugal to implement sanctions against the illegal regime in Southern Rhodesia" (paragraph 4 of Security Council resolution 320 (1972))

the essential aim was to ensure that all countries' imports to and exports from South Africa and the Portuguese Territories were confined to what is legitimate trade, that is, to goods and products which, in fact, originated in those Territories or were destined for them and were not disguised Rhodesian exports or imports. It had therefore sought in the Committee to co-operate in the refinement and adaptation of the proposals as originally submitted in such a way as to contribute towards the attainment of that objective; and accordingly welcomed the agreement that had been reached on the recommendations and suggestions in section III of the report which fell into that category and regretted that it could not endorse those proposals in section IV which did not.

56. Existing sanctions provisions were comprehensive in scope and, if fully applied by States professing to support sanctions, would eliminate the considerable volume of trade through South Africa and the Portuguese Territories. However, since existing provisions were not being adequately applied, it was useless to add new measures with no guarantee that they would be any more adequately enforced than the existing measures. Consequently, the United Kingdom delegation could not accept the proposals contained in paragraphs 23, 26, 31 and 32 in section IV. To that it should be added that some of the other proposals in that section involved technical issues, as well as matters relating to domestic law and international trade law, which had not been adequately considered by the Committee. Accordingly the United Kingdom delegation was unable to endorse them. Finally, the United Kingdom delegation wished to state that it had no objection to paragraphs 33 and 34 in section IV.

57. The delegation of the United States expressed appreciation to the delegations of Guinea, Kenya and the Sudan for the submission of their 24-point working paper. Though all the proposals in the working paper had not received unanimous approval, the paper played a very important role as the basis for the Committee's work. The United States was pleased that a number of the proposals had eventually been agreed on and hoped that those recommendations would lead to stricter and more widespread observance of sanctions. The United States had attempted to reduce the number of proposals on which agreement had not been reached by submitting alternatives that might have attracted the full support of the Committee and made the sanctions more effective.

58. The United States believed that the special report would have been best introduced if its first paragraph had incorporated paragraph 25 plus: "In addition, the Committee recommends that the Security Council request that where Member States' imports of the commodities specified above are greater than exports of these products to them as reported by South Africa, Angola or Mozambique,

such Member States should take all possible steps to ensure that none of these imports is of Rhodesian origin."

59. The representative of the United States noted his very strong reservations about paragraph 33 in its present form. Though supporting the program of sanctions established by Security Council resolution 253 (1968) and section III of the special report, the United States had to take into account its legislation concerning strategic materials. The United States wished to point out that discrepancies in statistics between trading countries could well indicate violations of the sanctions program. Investigation, however, could reveal that discrepancies were due to statistical error.

60. The Yugoslav delegation recalled the Yugoslav Government's position expressed in its note of 24 August 1972 to the Committee that "sanctions against Southern Rhodesia could be fully effective only if they were applied against Portugal and South Africa as well."[1]

---

[1]See document S/10852, paras. 51 and 52.

APPENDIX G: RHODESIA PROPOSALS FOR A
SETTLEMENT. PRESENTED TO PARLIAMENT BY THE
SECRETARY OF STATE FOR FOREIGN AND COMMON-
WEALTH AFFAIRS BY COMMAND OF HER MAJESTY,
NOVEMBER 1971 (COMMAND PAPER 4835)

Rhodesia

Report on Discussions with the Regime since
November 1970

The Five Principles
    1. Successive British Governments have been prepared to grant independence to Southern Rhodesia if certain essential requirements were met. These formed the basis of discussions with the Rhodesians during 1963 and 1964 and were subsequently formulated as the Five Principles. They are:

1. The principle and intention of unimpeded progress to majority rule, already enshrined in the 1961 Constitution, would have to be maintained and guaranteed.
2. There would also have to be guarantees against retrogressive amendment of the Constitution.
3. There would have to be immediate improvement in the political status of the African population.
4. There would have to be progress towards ending racial discrimination.
5. The British Government would need to be satisfied that any basis proposed for independence was acceptable to the people of Rhodesia as a whole.

Previous negotiations
    2. A series of negotiations conducted by the previous Administration with the Rhodesians failed to reach an agreement in accordance with these Principles.[1] Contacts were finally discontinued in May 1969.[2]

Subsequent developments in Rhodesia
    3. In a referendum in June 1969 the predominantly European electorate in Rhodesia endorsed proposals for a republican form of Government and a new Constitution. Shortly afterwards the Governor, Sir Humphrey Gibbs, obtained The Queen's permission to resign and

---

[1]Cmnd. 3159, Cmnd. 3171 and Cmnd. 3793.
[2]Cmnd. 4065.

both the British residual mission in Salisbury and its counterpart in London were withdrawn. The Republican Constitution had no legal status, but it was brought into effect by the Rhodesians on 2 March, 1970. Its main provisions are summarized at Annex A.

Her Majesty's Government's policy

4. When the present Government took office in June 1970, they confirmed their determination to seek a just and sensible solution to the Rhodesian problem in accordance with the Five Principles. For they recognized that while sanctions and international ostracism were having some effect on the economic situation in Rhodesia these measures had not brought about, nor seemed likely to bring about, the political changes that were confidently expected at the outset. Moreover, it was evident that the prospects for the African population as a whole could only deteriorate if the present situation remained unchanged. The economic, social and political advance of the Africans could take place only after a return to economic normality and the restoration of conditions in which orderly change would be possible. A settlement would open the way to a comprehensive aid and technical assistance program directed to expanding African opportunities in employment and education in the widest senses which would make an important contribution to this advance.

The exploratory exchanges

5. On 9 November, 1970 the Foreign and Commonwealth Secretary announced in the House of Commons that he had the previous week sent a preliminary message to Mr. Smith. This was the first of a series of written exchanges between the British Government and Mr. Smith designed to establish whether a basis for negotiations in accordance with the Five Principles could be found. These exchanges were sufficiently encouraging to justify further probing in greater depth. Thus in April 1971 Lord Goodman, assisted by a small team of senior officials, paid the first of four visits to Salisbury for detailed exploratory discussions. These visits continued at intervals throughout the summer and were concluded by a final found of talks at official level in October 1971. In the light of these discussions the British Government decided that a basis for negotiation with the Rhodesians had been established.

The negotiations

6. The Foreign and Commonwealth Secretary and the Attorney-General therefore flew to Salisbury on 14 November for these negotiations. While there they also held discussions with a wide cross-section of representative Africans and other leaders of opinion.

7. The subsequent negotiations at which the Rhodesian representatives were Mr. Ian Smith, Mr. Lardner-Burke and Mr. Howman led to provisional agreement being reached on proposals for a settlement. Both sides undertook to take steps to implement these proposals

provided that the British Government had first satisfied themselves that they would be acceptable to the people of Rhodesia as a whole. These proposals are set out in full at Annex B. A synopsis of the changes in Parliamentary representation, the franchise and the blocking mechanism which would arise from these proposals is given in the following paragraphs.

The proposed terms

8. The proposals for a settlement contain provisions which are summarized below under each of the Five Principles.

The First Principle. The 1969 Constitution expressly precludes the Africans from ever attaining more than parity of representation with the Europeans in the House of Assembly. It also relates any increase in African representation to the amount of income tax paid by the Africans. Under the proposed terms for a settlement, these provisions will be repealed and replaced by new provisions securing unimpeded progress to majority rule. The Africans will proceed to parity of representation in the House of Assembly through the creation of a new African higher roll, with the same income, property and educational qualifications as the European roll. As the numbers registered on this roll increase, additional seats will be created on a basis that will ensure that when parity of representation is reached the number of voters on the African higher and the European rolls will be approximately equal. The first two additional African members will be elected by the voters registered on the new African higher roll and the next two by indirect election under the existing system of Electoral Colleges, of Chiefs, Headmen and elected Councillors, and this sequence will be repeated in relation to further additional African members. By this means parity of representation will be reached with 50 European members and 50 African members in the House of Assembly. The latter will then comprise 24 indirectly elected, 18 directly elected by the new African higher roll and 8 directly elected, as at present, by the African lower roll. At this point a referendum will be held among all Africans registered on the two African rolls to decide whether or not the indirectly elected Africans should be replaced by directly elected Africans.

The Constitution will provide that, after the referendum and any elections necessary to give effect to the result, ten Common Roll seats will be created in the House of Assembly. After the result of this referendum has been implemented an independent Commission will be appointed to ascertain whether the creation of the Common Roll seats provided for in the Constitution is acceptable to the Rhodesian people at that time. But the adoption of any recommendation of this Commission to vary these arrangements will be a matter for the Rhodesian Parliament and will be subject to the normal procedure for amending specially entrenched provisions of the Constitution.

Failing any such agreed amendment, the Common Roll seats will be filled by an election in a single nationwide constituency by the voters on a roll consisting of all registered voters on the African higher and the European rolls. As the number of African voters increases, they will be able to determine the result of elections to a majority of these seats, thus achieving majority rule.

The Second Principle. At all stages in the progress to majority rule it will be necessary to obtain the approval of a substantial proportion of the African representatives in the House of Assembly for any amendment to the specially entrenched provisions of the Constitution which will include all the arrangements which affect African political advance. Until the Commission appointed after parity reports, such Constitutional amendments will require, in addition to a two-thirds majority of all the members of the House of Assembly and the Senate voting separately, the affirmative votes of a majority of the total European membership and of a majority of the total African membership in the House of Assembly. This will ensure that, in the unlikely event of all the indirectly elected Africans voting in favor of a retrogressive amendment to the specially entrenched provisions of the Constitution, the blocking mechanism will still rest in the hands of the directly elected African members of the Lower House. As African representation increases the two-thirds majority will require an increasing number of African votes. Thus after parity has been reached and the referendum on the future of the indirectly elected Africans has taken place, the need for an additional safeguard over and above the requirement of a two-thirds majority will disappear and it will be dropped. At this stage the support of at least 17 African members in the House of Assembly will be required to pass any amendment of a specially entrenched provision.

The Third Principle. The creation of the new African higher roll will bring with it the prospect in the near future of increased African representation in the House of Assembly. The reduction in the franchise qualifications for the existing African lower roll will enfranchise a large number of additional Africans. These two measures amount to a substantial improvement in the political status of the Africans. In addition there is provision for the British Government to allocate substantial sums of money for an aid program for Rhodesia over the next ten years in order to improve educational facilities for Africans and to help with the economic development of the Tribal Trust Lands, thus increasing job opportunities available for Africans. As a result of this aid the rate at which additional Africans will attain the income and educational qualifications required for the franchise will be accelerated. There will also be a new special Review of the cases of the remaining detainees by the existing Tribunal with a British observer present.

The Fourth Principle. There will be a new and strengthened Declaration of Rights, which will be enforceable in the courts (see Appendix III to Annex B). There will also be an independent Review Commission to examine forthwith the problem of racial discrimination in all fields, including the special problem of the allocation and use of land. The Rhodesians have undertaken to commend to Parliament legislation to give effect to the recommendations of this Commission subject to considerations that any Government would regard as overriding. Meanwhile they have made it clear that they are prepared to allocate additional land for African use as the need arises and have given an assurance that with the exception of a limited number of unauthorized occupants in certain areas, there will be no further evictions of Africans until the recommendations of the Review Commission have been considered.

The Fifth Principle. These proposals for a settlement will only be confirmed and implemented after the British Government have satisfied themselves that they are acceptable to the people of Rhodesia as a whole. Accordingly, the British Government have appointed a Commission with Lord Pearce as Chairman to canvass as thoroughly and as impartially as possible the views of all sections of Rhodesian opinion, including Rhodesians resident abroad or in detention. The Commission will start its work in the near future. Before and during this test of acceptability normal political activities will be permitted to the satisfaction of the Commission provided they are conducted in a peaceful and democractic manner. The Rhodesians will be releasing a substantial number of detainees. If the British Government are satisfied that the proposed terms are acceptable to the Rhodesian people as a whole, the Rhodesians will take the necessary steps to enact the legislative changes required to implement them. After these have been completed the British Government will recommend to Parliament that independence should be granted to Southern Rhodesia on this basis and that in these circumstances sanctions will no longer be required.

House of Commons, 80
House of Lords, 80
human rights, violations of, 73

Impunity, 73
India, 101
Indo-China, wars in, 22
Indonesia, 101
international law (see law)
international machinery, 91
Italy, 89-90

Japan, 74
Jessup, 25
Jet Aviation, 87
Joanna V, 48
Johannesburg, 64

Kairba North Power Scheme, 71
Kelsen, Hans, 37
Kenya, 22, 68, 96, 102
Kimberley, 4

Land Apportionment Act (1930),
  12, 17, 28
Law: International and Municipal,
  46, 76, 77, 83; Dualist and
  Monist School, 77
League of Nations, Covenant of,
  10-11, 14, 89
Leifflen, Roy, 101
Leopold II, King, 4-5
Lichtenstein, 87
Lisbon, 64, 87
Lloyds & Scottish Finance
  Company, 81
Lo Bengula, Chief, 6-8
London, 28-29, 31
Lourenco Marques, 64, 86, 93
Luanda, 64

McDowell, Carl, 101
Macmillan, 23
Malawi (formerly Nyasaland), 16
  30, 65

Malaya, 22
Manuela, 49
Monckton, Viscount, 16
Mozambique, 22, 100; port (see
  Lourenco Marques)
Moffat, John, 6
Mussolini, Benito, 91

Netherlands, 93; Bank of South
  Africa, 81
New York, 28
Nkomo, Joshua, 16, 30
Northern Rhodesia (see Zambia)
Nyasaland (now Malawi), 13, 15-16,
  30; Federation of Rhodesia and
  Nyasaland, 15
Nyerere, Julius, 32

Order in Council, 7-8, 17, 80
Orwell, George, 4

Panama, 101
Paris Peace Conference, 10
Peru, 101
Pierce Commission, 79
Plymouth, 48
Port Elizabeth, 81
Portugal, 4, 7, 22, 73
Prebisch, Raul, 99
Pretoria, 64
Privy Council, 80

Rhodes, Cecil John, 4, 6-8
Rhodesia, annexation to British
  Crown, 12; area, 3; constitution, 17; declaration of rights,
  17; federation of, 13, 15, 30;
  majority rule, 68; population, 3;
  self-government (Letters of
  Patent, 1 October 1923), 12;
  trade figures, 72
Rhodesian chrome ores and alloys,
  86
Rhodesian Electoral Act, 28
Rhodesian Front Party, 27, 30

Rhodesian exports and imports, 64
Rhodesian United Federal Party, 30
Rotenfels, 93
Rotterdam, 93
Royal Charter, 6
Rudd Concession, 6

St. Germain-en-Laye, 10
Salisbury, 16, 28, 31, 79, 87
sanctions: breaches of, 72; collective measures, 71; commissioner for, 99; economic, 89; extension of to South Africa and Portuguese territories, 100; fund, 98; implementation of, 95-96; judicial enforcement, 81; mandatory, 49-51, 68, 80, 91; rejection of, 72; violation of, 92
San Francisco Conference, 66
Scottish-Rhodesian Finance Ltd., 81
Sen, Mr. (Indian delegate to the Security Council), 71
Seydoux, Ambassador, 56
Sithole, Ndabaningi, 16, 30
Smith, Ian, 30-32, 79, 93
South Africa, 22, 26, 52, 73, 100
South West Africa, 22
Southern Rhodesia, 3, 15, 29; Act of (16 November 1965), 80
Soviet Union (see USSR)
Speer, Albert, 61
Stanley, 5
Stevenson, Ambassador (U.S.), 56
Strong, Maurice, 99
Sudan, 96, 102
Super Heater Co. Ltd., 81
Sweden, 93
Swiss Federal Council, 85
Swiss exports to and imports from Rhodesia, 86
Switzerland, 62, 74, 84-85, 87

Tanzania, 68

Territories, mandated and non-mandated, 11
"trade missions," 64
Transvaal, 3; Boers, 6
Treaty of Rome, 76
Treaties, Vienna Convention on the Law of, 62
Trujillo, 91
Trusteeship Council, 15
Turkey, 11; colonies, 11

UDI (Unilateral Declaration of Independence), 3, 47, 62, 78, 101
United Kingdom, 15, 22, 26, 68, 78, 93, 95, 102; Conservative and Labor government, 26, 31, 78; Minister of State of Foreign and Commonwealth Office, 71; Parliament, 17; Royal Navy, 101
United Nations, 28, 90
United Nations Association of the U.S., 84
United Nations Charter, Article 2, 3; Article 10, 40; Article 11, 40; Article 24, 38; Article 34, 63; Article 39, 38-39, 50; Article 40, 39; Article 41, 39, 48, 50, 80, 100; Article 42, 39; Article 49, 66; Article 50, 66; Article 73, 14-15, 42; Article 76, 23; Chapters XI, XII, and XIII, 14; Chapter VII, 90
United Nations General Assembly, 14-16, 20, 22, 25-26, 28, 30; Resolution 288 A (IV), 41; Resolution 377 A (V), 41; Resolution 500 (V), 41; Resolution 742 (VII), 16; Resolution 1514 (XV) granting of independence to colonial countries, 14 November 1960), 20, 22, 24, 26, 42; 1747 (XVI) (the Question of Southern Rhodesia, 28 June 1962), 20, 22, 24 26, 28, 46; 1807 (XVII), 41; 1899 (XVIII), 41; 2012 (XX) (the Ques-

tion of Southern Rhodesia, 12 October 1965), 32; 2022 (XX) (the Question of Southern Rhodesia, 5 November 1965), 33; 2024 (XX), (Question of Southern Rhodesia, 11 November 1965), 33; 2383 (XXIII), 52

United Nations General Assembly Special Committee on Information, 15

United Nations General Assembly Special Committee of Seventeen, 21

United Nations nonmembership, 63

United Nations Participation Act of 1945, 82

United Nations Security Council: 22, 30, 90; implementation of decisions by nonmember states, 84

United Nations Security Council Resolution 202 (first resolution on Rhodesia, 1965), 56; Resolution 217 (launched first stage in United Nations sanction policy, 1965), 48, 91, 101; Resolution 232 (imposed selective mandatory sanctions, 1966), 50, 57, 78, 81, 91; Resolution 253 (imposed comprehensive mandatory sanctions, 1968), 51, 57, 63-64, 70, 78, 81, 84-85, 87, 98; Resolution 277 (economic assistance to Zambia, 1970), 70; Resolution 314 (implementation of sanctions, 1972), 92; Resolution 318 (condemned all actions in violation of sanctions resolution, 1972), 57; Resolution 326 (established Security Council Special Mission, 1973), 68; Resolution 333, 102

United Nations Security Council Sanctions Committee: 80, 85, 91, 101; authority of, 93; political development of, 95; reports of, 72, 92, 95, 100; Special Mission, 68, 71

United States: 82-83, 102; Court of Appeals, 83; Grand Jury, 83; Supreme Court, 83

UNIVEX (Universal Exports Ltd.), 86

USSR, 71, 100-101

Vienna Convention on the Law of Treaties, 62

Washington, D.C., 64

Westminster, 16

Whitehall, 79

Whitehead, Prime Minister, 28, 30

White supremacy, 73

Wilhelmy & Co., Arnold (Johannesburg), 86

Wilson, Harold, 31-32, 78

World War I, 10

Yugoslavia, 101

Zambia, 3, 15-16, 30, 52, 68; assistance from British government, Scandanavian countries, UNDP, 66; foreign exchange costs of transporting imports and exports, 69

Zambian border, closure of, 67

Zambezi River, 6

Zimbabwe African National Union, 31

Zimbabwe African Peoples Union, 30

RALPH ZACKLIN was born in Leeds, England, obtained an LL.B. degree from London University, and took postgraduate degrees at Columbia University and the Graduate Institute of International Studies, Geneva. He joined the Carnegie Endowment staff in 1967 and became the Director of its International Law Program, a post he held until 1973. In this latter capacity, Dr. Zacklin was responsible for directing a wide-ranging program of research and training activities as well as the organizing of a number of international law conferences. In 1970 he was the Director of Studies at the Hague Academy of International Law.

Dr. Zacklin has written a number of books and articles including The Amendment of the Constitutive Instruments of the United Nations and Specialized Agencies and The Challenge of Rhodesia; he is the editor of The Changing Law of the Sea.

Dr. Zacklin joined the Office of Legal Affairs of the United Nations shortly after the completion of this study.